MOCK THE WEEK

1001

SCENES WE'D LIKE TO SEE

MOCK THE WEEK

1001

SCENES WE'D LIKE TO SEE

Ewan Phillips, Dan Patterson, Simon Bullivant,
Rob Colley, Dan Gaster, Ged Parsons, Giles Pilbrow,
Steve Punt and Colin Swash

BXTREE

First published in paperback 2010 by Boxtree
This edition published 2013 by Boxtree
an imprint of Pan Macmillan, a division of Macmillan Publishers Limited
Pan Macmillan, 20 New Wharf Road, London N1 9RR
Basingstoke and Oxford
Associated companies throughout the world
www.panmacmillan.com

ISBN 978-1-4472-6080-6

The material for this book is taken from
Mock the Week: Scenes We'd Like to See copyright © Not The Last Laugh Productions Ltd 2008,
first published 2008 by Boxtree;
and from *Mock the Week: This Year's Book* copyright © Not The Last Laugh Productions Ltd 2009,
first published 2009 by Boxtree.
This selection of Mock the Week one-liners copyright © Not The Last Laugh Productions Ltd 2010

A CIP catalogue record for this book is available from
the British Library.

Printed and bound by CPI Group (UK) Ltd, Croydon, CR0 4YY

Visit www.panmacmillan.com to read more about all our books
and to buy them. You will also find features, author interviews and
news of any author events, and you can sign up for e-newsletters
so that you're always first to hear about our new releases.

MOCK THE WEEK

1001

SCENES WE'D LIKE TO SEE

GREETINGS CARDS THAT WOULDN'T SELL

Sorry about your face

*Congratulations on putting
the death of your first wife behind you,
and remarrying*

*To a fine set of grandparents:
congratulations on your golden shower*

Now that you've lost your leg…

Congratulations on passing your STD test!

Good luck to the nicest paedophile we've ever worked with

Hope your paper cut heals soon

Royal Wedding 10th Anniversary

Congratulations, you're Minister for Trade and Industry

*Happy 12th birthday and
congratulations on the birth of your second child*

*Happy Cloning to you
and to you and to you*

Sorry to hear you're a hate-filled cleric

UNLIKELY DICTIONARY DEFINITIONS

bestiality (*noun*): an act of sexual congress with an animal, disgusting, you need help. Pervert. I don't know why I married you, I'm calling the police.

bird flu (*noun*): fictitious disease that will supposedly wipe out the Earth at any time soon, *see also*: SARS, ebola, flesh-eating virus, MRSA, global warming, nuclear war, grey goo, dirty bombs, supergun, ricin, dangerous dogs, Boris Johnson, etc.

catchasnatch (*noun*): 1. medieval dagger. 2. nickname for Roman emperor. 3. term used in graphic design . . . Frank Muir?

celebrity (*noun*): anyone.

dictionary (*noun*): book with words in, I imagine you already knew that or you wouldn't have bought this. Lifelong work for the likes of me, I'm not complaining, like, but obviously when I started out I wanted to be a novelist.

fart (*noun*): expulsion of trapped methane from the anus, possibly the funniest thing ever.

fisting (*verb*): what are you doing even looking this up?

fromage (*noun*): something which is smellier, uglier and more expensive in France, like their women.

leather (*noun*): material for garments, as in trousers and underwear, feels good, ooh, mmm.

miscagnate (*verb*): I've just no idea what this means, sorry.

misogynist (*noun*): someone who, for perfectly valid reasons, usually bitter experience, especially expensive divorce, hates women, they're all whores.

nadir (*noun*): the opposite of zenith, the lowest or most unsuccessful point, the ITV sitcom *Teenage Kicks*.

nipple clamp (*noun*): mine's killing me.

paedophile (*noun*): misunderstood, needlessly victimised, she told me she was sixteen.

poo (*noun*): 1. something you shit out, you can get big ones, runny ones or little pellet things (can be hard to flush). 2. Term of abuse, as in: 'That Hitler was a real poo.' 3. Sometimes with the suffix –f, meaning a gay man. (Shak) A poo, a poo, my kingdom for a poo (*Richard III*, Act V Scene 4). I think it's time I retired from this job . . . (Donne) No poo is an island, entire of itself. (Nurs rhyme) Humpty Dumpty sat on a poo. (Comic book) Batman & Poo. Endlessly amusing especially if you're a boy or if you spend all day writing a boring fucking dictionary. P.S. You're fired. (Editor.)

Ray Stubbs (*noun*): sexy beast, e.g. 'You turn me on like Ray Stubbs.'

verb (*verb*): a word that describes, you know, things, like, you know, verbs and stuff.

willy (*noun*): pfft, tee hee.

CARDS YOU NEVER SEE IN A NEWSAGENT'S WINDOW

FRENCH TUTOR:
GIVEZ-MOI UNE CALL MAINTENANT

MATHS TUTOR AVAILABLE 25/7.

WANT COCK? MEET ME OUTSIDE HERE
AT 2 A.M. ON TUESDAY.

WHAT ARE YOU LOOKING AT?

CAR BOOT. WOULD SUIT PERSON
WITH REST OF CAR.

BUILDER AVAILABLE AS SEEN ON TV (IN ITV'S
COWBOYS, CROOKS AND CONMEN).

ASK YOUR NEWSAGENT TO EXPLAIN
THE COMPLEXITIES OF THE CURRENT
GAZA CONFLICT.

CHILD MINDER AVAILABLE – HE MAY BE SMALL
BUT HE'S ROCK HARD.

LIKE ANTIQUES? SOME OF OUR CRISPS ARE
OVER TWO YEARS OLD.

SCHOOL CHILDREN:
JUST TWO AT A TIME PLEASE.
THERE'S ONLY SO MUCH OF ME
TO GO ROUND.

WALLCHARTS THE PAPERS DIDN'T GIVE AWAY

FAMOUS IN-THE-CLOSET HOMOSEXUALS

PEOPLE WHO WENT TO SCHOOL WITH MY MUM

FRUIT PASTILLE FLAVOURS

PENCIL STRENGTHS

ENVELOPE SIZES

MINISTERS FOR AGRICULTURE

GAY SEX PRACTICES

BURNS VICTIMS

GOITRES

LOVERS OF THE DUKE OF EDINBURGH

SPERM

VICTIMS OF FRED AND ROSE WEST

THE GUNS OF NAVARONE

LETTERS OF THE ALPHABET

UNLIKELY THINGS TO READ ON A MOTORWAY SIGN

SO I CAN TYPE ANYTHING IN HERE AND IT
COMES UP ON AN ELECTRONIC SIGN ON THE M6?
REALLY?

YUK – LOOK AT THAT, I THINK IT'S A FOX.
100 YARDS.

TIME TO JUNCTION 15: 28 MINUTES.
SEE IF YOU CAN DO IT IN 20.

MIKE ROBINSON WANTS TO BE YOUR FRIEND.
CONFIRM?

FUCK ALL OF YOU.

MEN SITTING IN STATIONARY JCBS
SMOKING AND READING THE *SUN*
FOR NEXT 29 MILES.

YOU THOUGHT YOU'D GOT RID OF ME
WHEN WE WERE DIVORCED BUT
I'M STILL WATCHING YOU.

DON'T DRIVE TIRED. PULL IN FOR
A RED BULL AND VODKA AT JUNCTION 8.

HONK IF YOU'VE HAD IT TODAY.

MAJOR ROADWORKS AHEAD.
EXPECT DELAYS UNTIL 2065.

NO OVERTAKING.
NO BLACKS. NO IRISH. NO DOGS.

BEWARE: PEOPLE DRIVING LIKE C*NTS AHEAD.

LIVERPOOL 6, MANCHESTER 8.
HA! TAKE THAT, RAFA!

DANGER: FOG.
SHROUDING THE ROAD AHEAD
LIKE GREAT WHITE FURS, SLIPPING STEALTHILY
DOWN FROM THE CROW-BLACK SHOULDER-LIKE
EMBANKMENTS ON TO THE ENDLESSLY
UNRAVELLING DAMASK OF THE
MOTORWAY.

FIRST-DRAFT LINES FROM
GREAT NOVELS

My father's family name being Pirrip and my Christian name being Philip meant I had a shit time at school.

It is a truth universally acknowledged that a single man in possession of a good fortune must be beating off the pussy with a stick.

It was a bright, cold day in April and the clock struck thirteen. 'Big Ben's on the fucking blink again,' sighed Winston Smith.

When Mr Bilbo Baggins of Bag End announced that he would shortly be celebrating his eleventy-first birthday, most readers thought 'This sounds shit' and put the book back on the shelf.

It was a dark and stormy night, the rain fell in torrents so I just stayed in and watched telly.

Last night I dreamt I went to Spearmint Rhino again.

'It was the gardener,' said Poirot, 'and over the next 374 pages I will explain how.'

Marley was dead, which was a real pisser for the Wailers.

Call me Ishamel, or u can txt me if u like. Dat wd be betta. Lol Ahab x

'Christmas won't be Christmas without any presents,' grumbled Jo. 'Well tough shit,' said Father, contemplating wrapping the ungrateful little sod up in the rug and setting it on fire.

All children except one grow up. Poor Peter Pan had a congenital kidney disorder, meaning he was stuck at 4ft 3ins.

Lolita, light of my life, bait of my jail.

I am an invisible man and unfortunately, I write in invisible ink.

'Tom!' No answer. 'Tom!' No answer. 'Tom–'
   'For fuck's sake, I'm having a shit!' shouted Tom Sawyer.

As Gregor Samsa awoke one morning, he found himself transformed in his bed into a giant insect. However when he rang work Ken, his line manager, said, 'Right, Samsa, I've had enough of this bollocks: you're fired.'

Alice was beginning to get very bored of sitting by her sister on the riverbank, so she checked no one was around, hit her with a stone and pushed her into the water.

Here is Edward Bear coming downstairs now, bump bump bump on the back of his head behind Christopher Robin. 'Let that be a lesson to you, Edward. Mr Robin doesn't like grasses,' said Christopher.

It was the best of times, yup, it really was the best of times.

Emma Woodhouse was handsome, clever and rich with a comfortable home and happy disposition, but she was gagging for cock.

The drought had lasted for ten million years and the reign of the terrible lizards had long since ended, but still I was in a priority queue and all the operators were busy.

Once upon a time there were four little rabbits: Flopsy, Mopsy, Shagger and Deep Throat.

UNLIKELY HOROSCOPES

♓ PISCES *Feb 21–March 20* Hitler will invade Poland in 1939.

♈ ARIES *March 21–April 20* You will see a man, or possibly a woman, unless you don't leave the house maybe.

♉ TAURUS *Apr 21–May 21* Like your star sign, Taurus, this is bull.

♊ GEMINI *May 22–Jun 22* A stranger will come into your midst and cause an accident or expire at your feet (this applies only to people who live in the TV programme *Casualty*).

♋ CANCER *June 23–July 23* Soon Cancer won't just be your star sign.

♌ LEO *July 24–Aug 23* You will regret having wasted 45 pence and about twenty seconds of your day any time around about . . . now, there you go, told you.

♍ VIRGO *Sept 24–Oct 23* The letter you are expecting will be late.

♏ SCORPIO *Oct 24–Nov 22* The winning lottery numbers will be 7, 9, 17, 24, 29 and 33, though this may be a week out of date.

♐ SAGITTARIUS *Nov 23–Dec 21* All Sagittarians are c*nts.

♑ CAPRICORN *Dec 22–Jan 20* Is this the card you were thinking of?

≋ AQUARIUS *Jan 21–Feb 19* You are being fooled by an overpaid charlatan who started out as a sports reporter, but realised where the real money is.

⟓ PISCES *Feb 21–March 20* You will meet a dark stranger today, particularly if you live in Africa.

♈ ARIES *March 21–April 20* You are a closet homosexual.

♉ TAURUS *Apr 21–May 21* You should go to your bedroom window and stand there naked for a minute, then turn around and stay there for another minute, you should do this especially if your name is Mrs Hughes and you live at 56, The Avenue, Clapham . . . around 3.30 would be best for me.

♊ GEMINI *May 22–Jun 22* Mercury is prominent today, so don't drink tap water.

♋ CANCER *June 23–July 23* You are about to have a brilliant week, but after reading this you will remember nothing.

♌ LEO *July 24–Aug 23* Look out for an old lady on a zebra crossing this morning . . . oops, too late.

♍ VIRGO *Sept 24–Oct 23* There is a gun trained on you, Virgo; now stay still, don't try anything and no one will get hurt, understand?

♏ SCORPIO *Oct 24–Nov 22* Today you will feel much better/worse [delete as applicable]

♐ SAGITTARIUS *Nov 23–Dec 21* You are a gullible person.

13

UNSUCCESSFUL PERSONAL ADS

Men seeking women / Women seeking men

Me: short, hairy, fat, pigeon fancier. You: will probably already have moved on.

Ex-rugby player, dark, swarthy, square jawed, broad shouldered, 6′3″, hands like shovels, all woman.

Fun loving, wacky, crazy gal looking for man to share the good times, I'm mad me, all me friends say so, honest, I love you already I can tell, wooo arrrghhh waaaa.

Just back from extremely long time in foreign country. Looking for woman with low profile. Love children.

Hermaphrodite with flaming red hair, three beautiful legs, one eye, broken nose, no teeth seeks similar.

Widow, 56, likes opera and cinema. Seeks professional male for long country walks, candlelit dinners and eye-watering anal sex.

Companion required for long sessions of Sudoku. No timewasters.

Long-term gay man, looking to get back 'out there', no STDs, once bitten and all that.

Bride with six sisters seeks man from large family.

Outspoken monoped, recently divorced, looking for ageing millionaire for long hops in the country.

Dull, unimaginative and unadventurous person seeks soulmate. Won't travel.

They said I should never be released, they said I am a danger to women, let's prove them wrong . . .

Me: curvy, great sense of humour, loves food, larger than life, positive, enjoys cooking, dining out, bubbly personality. You: must like a fat lass.

Me: man. You: woman preferably.

Man with ADD seeks woman for companionship, fun, long . . . ooh look, car for sale, £1,500!

Dastardly cad seeks lonely, wealthy spinster with understanding solicitor for exertion-filled final few months.

Straight man seeks comedian with jokes after death of funny half of double act.

Were you that man on the tube last week? I was that woman. Call me! Anon.

Caveman seeks match.

Man seeks man willing to kill and eat him or, if not, for theatre, days out in the country and pub quizzes.

Were you the blonde running fast on Hampstead Heath at 9.30 on Tuesday night? I was the man in the black balaclava running close behind. Wish we'd had chance to talk. Call me.

THINGS YOU WON'T HEAR IN A
RADIO TRAFFIC REPORT

'Unless you clear the M25, Chris Moyles gets it.'

'And there is now a 20-mile tailback caused by the wreckage of my helicopter.'

Beep! 'Same to you, you fat twat, learn how to drive!'

'There is currently a queue of four cars at the traffic lights on the High Street.'

'There's pandemonium below me, fire, smoke, loud bangs . . . we appear to be flying over Helmand. Steve, what are you bloody doing?'

'Mrs Jones is currently waiting for the bin lorry to move from the middle of Fir Tree Avenue.'

'. . . and a message to Dave back in the studio: Dave, if you put on James Blunt one more time, we're going to strafe your mum's house.'

'And from this helicopter, I can clearly see my urine splashing on the roofs of the cars queuing on the M5.'

'Some old bastard is attempting to reverse park his Volvo outside Pizza Express, he's never going to get it in there, stay with me and we'll see if he does.'

'It's only taken me two minutes to get to Tower Bridge this morning, but then I am in a helicopter.'

'Don't go on the M25 between Junctions 7 and 11 tonight, it is absolutely bumper-to-bumper, all four lanes closed. OK, we off air, Jim? Great, that should leave my journey home clear again.'

'And hilariously, on the van in front someone has written: "I wish my wife was as dirty as this" in the dirt on the back door. Brilliant.'

'Traffic report and I'm in a fucking helicopter, no one told me this, I hate heights.'

'So, carnage on the M1, at least ten people dead. Here's Katie Melua.'

'If you're on the North Circular heading towards Palmers Green, watch out by the Asda, there's a woman waiting to cross with amazing tits.'

'If you're heading south clockwise on the M25, what the fuck are you doing, you maniac? You're going to cause a crash!'

'As we put on "Ride of the Valkyries", we're going to swoop down and take out some gooks with a chopper.'

'They look like ants down there, oh, apparently they are ants, we haven't taken off yet.'

'Sometimes when I am up here circling, gazing down at the cars trundling along the highways, I have this overwhelming urge just to ram this fucker into a building.'

'Launch missile. Fire 1!'

'We have problems on the M1, M3, M4, M6 and M11 – and that concludes tomorrow's traffic report.'

'Traffic slow below me – mainly as they're watching me bungee jumping out of this helicopter.'

UNLIKELY THINGS TO READ ON A MOTORWAY SIGN

TITS. POO. WANK. BALLS. OOPS, IS THIS ON?

YOU'RE LATE. GET A MOVE ON. QUICK!

TOM STOPPARD'S BEST WORK IS
BEHIND HIM NOW. DISCUSS.

SPEED CAMERAS WITH NO FILM IN AHEAD.

DO THE OPPOSITE OF WHAT THE SIGN SAYS
FOR THE NEXT 100 MILES.

TEAR IN SPACE-TIME CONTINUUM AHEAD.

SPEED CAMERAS AHEAD. WOMEN WITH
THEIR TITS OUT GET LET OFF.

EDGE OF CLIFF AHEAD.
TOO LATE TO SLOW DOWN.

TODAY'S SPEED RESTRICTIONS WERE
BROUGHT TO YOU BY POWERGEN.

SIMON SAYS SLOW DOWN AND
MOVE TO THE CENTRE LANE.

WATCHING ALL THESE CARS DRIVING PAST
MAKES ME HORNY.

IS THAT REALLY THE FASTEST
THAT PIECE OF SHIT CAN GO?.

PLACE WHERE THAT BLOKE FROM *'ALLO'ALLO!*
CRASHED AHEAD.

ICE ON ROAD AHEAD.
HAVE FUN. FEEL ALIVE.
LIVE DANGEROUSLY.

IF YOU DON'T WANT TO KNOW THE RESULT
OF TONIGHT'S UEFA CUP SEMI-FINAL,
LOOK AWAY NOW.

I AM THE GHOST OF YOUR
DRIVING INSTRUCTOR.
ONLY YOU CAN READ THIS.
I WILL HAVE MY VENGEANCE.

REJECTED EXAM QUESTIONS

1. Put these queens of England in the order you would shag them.

2. Paul has a cake. He gives Peter 4/9 of it, he gives Mary 1/12 of it, he then gives Barry 2/7 of it and Frances the rest. Can you diagnose which mental illness he is clearly suffering from?

3. In nothing did Louis XIV err more than his policy on the Church. Illustrate using potato prints and glitter.

4. Will this exam paper be marked before the end of the summer holidays? Discuss.

5. *Mansfield Park* is set neither in Mansfield nor a park. What the fuck is Jane Austen on about?

6. Using the weapon provided, run amok in the exam room making reference to the government, Jesus and your over-protective parents.

7. Black music is better than white music. Diss.

8. When in Rome, you see a man shit in the street. What should you do?

9. Complete the following line of poetry: 'There was a young man from Bangkok . . .'

10. Discuss Shakespeare's use of the word 'c*nt' in Romeo and Juliet.

11. Terry has translated Hamlet's soliloquy, changing all the letter Bs to Cs, and Anne has translated Coleridge's *Kubla Khan*, replacing all As with Ts. How much of their lives has been a waste?

12. Cakes are nice, aren't they?

13. Draw a diagram of the female reproductive organs using the sheets provided to wipe up your jizz afterwards.

14. My dog has got no nose. Please show how it smells using a diagram.

15. John travels 5 miles to work where he earns £10. Can't he do better than that?

16. How many sexual partners have you had? Please give details in your answer.

17. Henry VIII's wives got what they deserved by and large. Discuss without using the word 'slags'.

18. Everything in history is Britain's fault. Agree.

19. If John earns £300 and buys a DVD for £100, how much was he ripped off?

20. If George takes 65 tablets and Sally swallows 25 tablets, how good is your alibi going to have to be?

21. If John has five potatoes and Colin has four, how long before Channel 4 makes a documentary about them called *Jamie's Potato Addicted Teens*?

LINES YOU'D NEVER SEE IN A JAMES BOND BOOK

'We're very proud of this little gadget, it means you can plug things in all over Europe,' beamed Q.

Bond looked into the Austrian's eyes. 'Your go,' Stumpf said coldly, confident he had won games like this, in casinos like this, against men like Bond a million times. A bead of sweat formed on Bond's lip as he made his move with an affected nonchalance. 'Snap,' he said, and lit a cigarette.

Groaning and exhausted, Bond summoned his last strength and released one hand from behind his back, moving it with practised ease to the packet of Rennie's in his pocket.

Fighting his fatigue, Bond pressed a button on his keyboard. His heart pounded as the message came up: 'Goldfinger has added you as a friend on Facebook'.

'He may not look like much, Bond, but he's got a sharp, poisoned implant in his cock, so don't let him fuck you.'

'That's funny,' said Bond wistfully. 'My mother's name was Pussy Galore too.'

Bond eased out of his Kappa tracksuit bottoms, removed his Burberry baseball cap and placed his Aquascutum jumper on the bed. He was alone in his apartment and enjoying catching up with *Britain's Hardest Pubs* on Sky One over a 'chow mein' Pot Noodle.

CARDS YOU NEVER SEE IN A NEWSAGENT'S WINDOW

CAR FOR SALE: SEE BELOW
(OWNER LOST CONTROL AND DROVE INTO
THE NEWSAGENT'S WINDOW).

I AM GENUINELY NEW IN TOWN AND INTERESTED
IN MAKING FRIENDS AND SEEING THE SIGHTS.
NB: I'M A PRE-OP TRANSSEXUAL WHO IS
A PROSTITUTE. RING THIS NUMBER.

ILLEGAL IMMIGRANTS WANTED FOR
POTENTIALLY LETHAL AGRICULTURAL JOBS.
MEET ME HERE 3.30 A.M. NEXT TUESDAY.

ODD BLOW JOB MAN – NO KNOB TOO SMALL.

CHURCH FATE: PROBABLY EVENTUAL CLOSURE
DUE TO APATHY AND DEVELOPMENT INTO
LUXURY FLATS . . .

ROOM TO RENT IN LARGE
CENTRAL LONDON TOWNHOUSE
WITH THREE LESBIAN NYMPHOMANIAC
SUPERMODELS, £50 PW.

CAR FOR SALE.
RED ONE WITH FOUR WHEELS.
ONE LADY OWNER.

UNLIKELY SIGNS

WARNING! CHEESE

CAUTION CROSSING CHILDREN
– THEY'VE PROBABLY GOT KNIVES, KEEP YOUR DOORS LOCKED

IF YOU CAN READ THIS YOU'RE GAY

PLEASE DO NOT SHIT ON THE SEATS

WATCH OUT . . . TOO LATE

NO SIGNS FOR 50 MILES

IN CASE OF EMERGENCY – INFORM SUPERMAN

WARNING: FALLING STOCKBROKERS

DANCE CLASS AHEAD – SLOW, SLOW, QUICK QUICK SLOW

PLEASE DO NOT TAKE THE OPPORTUNITY TO
ENJOY YOURSELF IN THIS POOL

PLEASE IGNORE THIS SIGN

WHEN BLACK FLAG IS VISIBLE, GO IN THE SEA IF YOU MUST,
BUT DON'T SAY WE DIDN'T WARN YOU

WARNING: YOU ARE BEING SURVEYED BY CAMERA,
THIS WILL CONTINUE FOR 24 HOURS, EVEN WHEN YOU
LEAVE HERE AND GO HOME

GREETINGS CARDS THAT WOULDN'T SELL

Sorry to hear the condom split

Happy new breasts!

From an aunt who doesn't know you very well

Wishing you a very happy fatwa

Congratulations on your first ejaculation

Kim Jong, sorry to hear you're Il

To a special 'Uncle'

*Congratulations on your one-month wedding anniversary
– we all gave it two weeks*

Thank you for swallowing

Sorry to hear you're now on the sex offenders' register

Now you are One
(contains message inside: *Congratulations on coming out!*)

Congratulations on your regime change
(also available: *So sorry to hear you've been toppled*)

At last you've passed a solid!

UNLIKELY THINGS TO READ ON A MOTORWAY SIGN

NICE COMBOVER, SLAPHEAD

SOME OF THE FOLLOWING SIGNS
CONTAIN STRONG LANGUAGE AND
SCENES OF A SEXUAL NATURE

THERE MAY BE TROUBLE AHEAD.
PREPARE TO FACE MUSIC AND DANCE.

HUGE FATAL CRASH HERE ON 25 APRIL.
LET ME KNOW IF YOU CAN MAKE IT.

LAST CHANCE TO MISS EXIT FOR FIVE MILES

WELCOME TO CONE WORLD THEME PARK

EIGHT-LANE MOTORWAY WIDENING PROJECT
AHEAD – FIVE LANES SHUT

CAUTION: CRACKS IN BUILDERS' ARSES AHEAD

SERVICES 1 MILE – CLEAN SERVICES 25 MILES

TEDIOUS GAME OF 'I SPY' NEXT 100 MILES

VELCOME TO ZE AUTOBAHN – PLEAZ DRIVE
LIKE EIN LUNATIC

CAUTION: BADLY PLANNED SIGN AHE

EXPECT DELAYS.
DON'T KNOW WHERE OR WHEN,
JUST EXPECT THEM

DUE TO LACK OF CAT'S EYES,
BEWARE DWARVES PEEPING OUT OF HOLES,
WEARING SILVER CONTACT LENSES

WORRYING TYRE FRAGMENTS
– NEXT 200 YARDS

HUGELY DISAPPOINTING THEME PARK:
2 MILES

PICNIC AREA AND SHALLOW GRAVE SITE

SINISTER HITCH-HIKERS NEXT 5 MILES

UNLIKELY LINES FROM A
POLITICAL BIOGRAPHY

We had to leave Downing Street in a hurry that night, because the body in the boot was beginning to smell. A hard night's digging lay ahead of us. 'This is no job for a Cabinet minister,' I said. He laughed, picked up the shovel and spat on his hands.

'What ho, Jeeves! Appoint Gussie Fink-Nottle as my head of security,' said Boris.

Silently, I withdrew from my panting secretary, zipped up me trousers and bit into a nearby sausage roll.

'The Conservatives are fuck all,' I thought, as my fist sank into the doughy nose of David Cameron and my foot sprang into the boyish crotch of George Osbourne.

'Your Highness, it's done,' I said, and turned away from the tunnel and into the dark Parisian night, throwing my mobile and the blinding flashlight into the Seine.

I am an invisible man, but that's inevitable when you are Shadow Agriculture Minister.

Our eyes met across the Mansion House table. He was in a daring lounge suit, standing out amongst the white tie and stiffness. He winked and seemed to do a funny breathing thing with his mouth. I could tell he wanted me, so I went over and asked his name. 'Brown, Gordon Brown,' he said, breathily.

THIS IS GEORGE BUSH. LOOK. PRESIDENT. LOOK. WAR. OOOH. PRETZEL. LOOK. THE END.

As the wife, spouse, partner, confidante, soul mate and motivator of Tony Blair, I never expected, supposed, considered, guessed, that one day the Hachette Publishing Company would ask, request, cajole, persuade, force me to write a book, volume, autobiography, memoir, but they said they'd pay by the word.

The scent and smoke and sweat of a negotiating chamber are nauseating at three in the morning, thought Ban Ki Moon.

'You're more than just a great Chancellor,' said the Prime Minister. Suddenly, he was on top of me and I felt his mouth against mine.

In my case, MP also stood for massive paedophile.

Clare Short – nah, Harriet Harman – possibly if she didn't speak, Hazel Blears – filthy, Jacqui Smith – phwoar! Caroline Flint – tasty, but like a bag of potatoes in the sack.

it wuzzz nt eezie to mayke itt two the top wiv me lurnin difffi-culltyes

Call me Prescott.

Vlad Putin and the Prisoner of Azerbaijan: Chapter Two.

I Shot JFK and Other Hunting Accidents by Dick Cheney

GREETINGS CARDS THAT WOULDN'T SELL

To a very special stepson by my second marriage,
on the occasion of your gay wedding

Sorry you failed your driving test.
See you at the pedestrian's funeral

Happy 143rd Birthday

Sorry for your very sad loss. Who's getting his laptop?

Congratulations on your first affair!
Pay a hundred quid to this address or the photos go public

Happy Birthday, Sweet Sixteen
– you can now wear this badge:
'I'm Legal'

Sorry to hear you're dead

Happy Anniversary! Who'd have thought it's a year since
your family were all killed in that tragic accident?

Thank you for that night of passion.
I think I've given you chlamydia

Congratulations on your divorce. I never liked him

Commiserations,
you've got breast/testicular/prostate cancer
(delete as appropriate)

UNLIKELY SIGNS

CAUTION: MISLEADING SIGN

NO RUNNING, NO JUMPING, NO FUCKING UP THE ARSE

STAND CLEAR OF THE DOORS – THE LOCK'S A BIT DODGY,
THEY COULD OPEN AT ANY TIME

BY ORDER OF HM GOVT, IF YOU'RE HAPPY AND YOU KNOW IT,
YOU MUST CLAP YOUR HANDS

PLEASE DO NOT KISS THE ANIMALS

YOU DON'T HAVE TO BE MAD TO WORK HERE – BECAUSE THAT
WOULD BE AN IRRESPONSIBLE EMPLOYMENT PRACTICE

GOLF SALE SIGN SALE 200 YARDS

CAUTION: GUARD DOGS. AND ONCE THEY CATCH YOU,
THEY'LL WANT TO PLAY FETCH FOR HOURS

UNATTENDED LUGGAGE WILL BE TAKEN AWAY,
RIFLED THROUGH AND THEN PUT BACK

STAND WELL BACK FROM THE PLATFORM EDGE,
IF YOU'RE TRYING TO COMMIT SUICIDE,
A RUN UP'S ALWAYS BEST

BRITAIN WELCOMES CHEAP HARD-WORKING POLES

LINES YOU WOULDN'T FIND IN A HARRY POTTER BOOK

This is a true story.

'So you killed your own parents, Harry?'

'You were better than Ron,' said Harry as he withdrew from Hermione and lit a cigarette.

'My work here is done,' said Harry before flying away.

Hermione crawled from the rubble suffering from the effects of the bomb's radiation.

Mr and Mrs Potter didn't want Harry, so they dreamt up an incredible cover story to get rid of him . . .

So, evil had triumphed.

'Death to the West!' shouted Voldemort as the flames licked Hogwarts.

'I like it here in the Shire,' said the Hobbit.

At last it dawned on Ron: with all his magic powers, he didn't have to be ginger any more.

And Harry begat Zorab . . .

Harry Potter, the boy who never grew up thanks to a rare genetic condition . . .

'You've only got one GCSE, Harry. What the bloody hell have you been doing for the last seven years?'

Logging on to YouTube, Harry watched the flickering images of fundamentalists finishing off Nearly Headless Nick . . .

According to the *Daily Express*, first-time buyers like Hagrid are being priced out of the market.

The rafters creaked eerily as Harry's lifeless corpse swung to and fro on the end of a frayed noose. 'A classic case of too much, too young,' said Snape.

'Have you heard? The police have taken away Dumbledore's hard drive!'

'Have you noticed the resemblance between Hagrid and Robbie Coltrane?' asked Hermione.

'I've turned my cock into a frog!' Ron exclaimed.

It was Harry's eighteenth birthday, and he slipped on his Nazi uniform, ready for the party.

'Where's Ron?' asked Harry. 'He flew his broomstick into the engine of an F17,' said Hermione.

'Oh no, Ron Weasley's hanged himself because he couldn't pay back his student loan.'

'Pass the tissues, Harry,' said Ron.

'Class, here's your new master of the dark arts, Mr Daniels.'

So that's that, there is no God.

WALLCHARTS THE PAPERS DIDN'T GIVE AWAY

THE GRAND OLD DUKE OF YORK'S MEN

VITAL BRITISH MILITARY SECRETS

STARS OF THE UNIBOND LEAGUE

STOOL SAMPLES

WEATHER PRESENTERS OF THE TYNE-TEES REGION

STARS OF THE SEX OFFENDERS REGISTER

PEBBLES OF THE WORLD

THE SPECTACLES OF JOHN MAJOR

ROYAL AUTOPSIES

CONKERS

THE AL-QAEDA HIT LIST

BRITISH NEWSPAPERS' FREE WALLCHARTS

BIRD EXCREMENT

THE DULUX COLOUR CHART

UNLIKELY CONCERTS

*Britney Spears and Amy Winehouse
drink Magners and improvise*

The Al-Qaeda Singers

Ann Widdecombe vs the Pussycat Dolls

Gordon Brown's 'Songs from the Shows'

The Dreamers minus Freddie, a capella

Heather Mills and Yoko Ono Sing the Beatles

Cliff Richard in Silent Prayer

Chesney Hawkes – My Fifty Greatest Hits

Michael Barrymore and Friends

Gerry Without his Pacemaker

St Winnifred's School Choir Sing Napalm Death

Gary Glitter and the Minipops

*Class 3C perform 'The Golden Hour of
Beginner's Recorder Classics'*

The Rolling Stones 'This Really Is It, This Time' tour

Kim Jong Il Sings Shirley Bassey

LETTERS IGNORED BY *JIM'LL FIX IT*

Dear Jim, I am a fifteen-year-old boy scout and am desperate to see a real-life pair of tits, what can I do?

Dear Jim, I am an unpopular African dictator and am about to have an election, could you fix it for me?

Dear Jim, can you fix it? I can, love Bob the Builder.

Dear Jim, can you kill Princess Diana and make it look like an accident? Love Phil and Liz, London.

Dear Jim, can you fix it for me to become a TV presenter despite having no obviously discernible talent and just a funny voice, odd hair, terrible dress-sense and a habit of smoking cigars constantly?

Hi Jim, our cat's a randy bastard – can you fix him?

Dear Jim, now then now then, guys and gals, have a letter here, howzabout that then, ladies and gents, Dr Magic, very busy man, special chair, goodness gracious me, young lady, clunk-click, this is the age of the train, pop that badge on there like that, champ, Top of the Pops. Love from Jim there you see.

Dear Jim, I would like to spend some time in the company of a bizarre octogenarian and the wardrobe of his long-dead mother. Could you fix it for me?

Dear Jim, I was a cub scout featured on your programme in the 1980s, and due to a faulty seat belt have been strapped into a fucking rollercoaster for the last twenty-six years. Can you fix it for me to be rescued?

Dear Jim, I have just won the football pools so I don't have to work answering the mail on your shit show any more.

UNLIKELY SIGNS

NO PARKING – SHITTING PIGEONS ABOVE

NO LAUGHING, SMILING OR WAVING

WORKMAN'S CLOTHES MUST BE WORN IN THIS GAY BAR

'KEEP BRITAIN OUT OF EUROPE' MEETING
– 5 KILOMETRES

DANGER: SHARKS! JUST KIDDING. OR ARE WE?

IN CASE OF VANDALISM – BREAK GLASS

DO NOT FEED THE FERN BRITTON

CAUTION: TIME WARP AHEAD/BEHIND YOU

CAUTION: READING SIGNS ON MOTORWAY
MAY CAUSE ACCIDENTS

AREA OF OUTSTANDING NATURAL BEAUTY
OBSCURED BY SIGN

FOR LAND OF OZ – FOLLOW YELLOW BRICK ROAD

PLEASE DO NOT FEED THE ANIMALS,
WE'RE TRYING TO STARVE THEM TO DEATH

LINES YOU'D NEVER SEE IN A
JAMES BOND BOOK

'No, Mr Bond, I expect you to shit yourself!'

'James, he's using the diamonds to divert a giant laser onto New York from outer space.' Bond took the bottle out of M's shaking hand and helped her off the floor into bed.

'Now pay attention 007, this looks like an ordinary suitcase, but if you push this button, a handle comes out and you can wheel it.'

Bond left the casino. He always knew when he was tired, because he tended to nod off and piss himself.

Bond shut the door, locked it and with a tired sigh sat down on the bed. He took out his mascara and began to apply it.

Bond slid out of her and, checking she was asleep, noiselessly wiped his cock on the curtains.

'Flush, you bastard,' said Bond coldly, but the floater just stared back at him from the bowl.

'M should stand for Minge,' Bond said as he went down on her.

He was an educated man from a great family, a man of sophisticated tastes at the top of his profession and yet, as he began his task, the thought nagged away at him: he was now no more than a mercenary, a blunt tool used by forces more powerful than himself for their own ends. The great things he might have done – could still do – would forever now be devalued. 'Fuck it, think of the money!' said Sebastian Faulks.

BAD FIRST INTERVIEW QUESTIONS

'You were lucky to get a point there eh, Sir Alex?'

'So I can get swine flu simply by doing this to this pig?'

'Jordan, can you just sing a bit of it for us now?'

'Could you drive me to where you were keeping the British journalist hostage?'

'Are you trying to seduce me, Miss Widdecombe?'

'And for your first record, Mr bin Laden?'

'Do you mind if I take off my trousers?'

'Got any gear, Mr Cameron?'

'Do you swallow?'

'Wayne Rooney, in your opinion – *The Golden Notebook* excepted – does Doris Lessing's oeuvre truly merit a Nobel Prize?'

'Are you happy with a verdict of accidental death, Mr al Fayed?'

'Have you seriously never even had just one wank, Your Holiness?'

'Prince Harry, why have you got such thick red hair when all the other men in your family are balding?'

'Can I ask you to say all that again? My pen ran out.'

UNLIKELY PUB NAMES

The Dog & Toddler

The Hostile Atmosphere

The Entirely White Clientele

The Slapper & Husband

The Hostage's Head

The Chapped Arse

The Strange Smell

The Gary Glitter

The Bottled Face

The Cock & Blister

The Southern Poof

The Keg of Piss

The Undercooked Chicken

The Missile & Duck

The Unsanitary Toilets

The Legionnaires' Outbreak

The Stray Dart

The Queen's Impending Death

Vlad the Impaler

The Maggot & Sandwich

The Pair of Tits

COMPUTER GAMES THAT WOULDN'T SELL

MORTGAGE BROKER III

SONIC THE SURVEYOR

PRO-EVOLUTION CROWN GREEN BOWLS

WOMB RAIDER

SUPER MILIBAND BROTHERS

POKAMOM

DONKEY DONG

GRAND THEFT HANDBAG

PARLIAMENTARY MOTION

DOGGER

REMAINS OF THE DAY: THE GAME

SEX CRIME 2: TOKYO

LUIGI'S BUNGALOW

TONY HAWK'S PRO FRIDGE CARRIER

TEACH YOURSELF WALLOON

STREET RACING: GRIFTERS

FLY SWATTER 2

LINES YOU WOULDN'T FIND IN A HARRY POTTER BOOK

'Harry,' said Ron awkwardly, 'have you seen *Brokeback Mountain*?'

'I'm afraid your scar has turned malignant, Mr Potter,' said the doctor.

Harry slowly unzipped his trousers . . .

Harry turned to Tigger and said, 'I'm sorry, I appear to be in the wrong book.'

It wasn't only Harry's feet that stuck out from his cloak of invisibility, as he sneaked into the girls' changing room.

The inspector from Ofsted pulled up outside Hogwarts . . .

'Imagine that,' said Harry as he stepped out of the shower. 'It was just a dream after all.'

'Once you've had a muggle, you'll never go back,' said Hermione.

Slowly the car carrying J.R.R. Tolkien's literary executor pulled up outside Hogwarts.

Harry tightened the belt around his arm, slapped up a vein and as he injected said, 'Now that is magic.'

Harry had always known he was a woman trapped inside a man's body.

Ron and Harry smiled as the Coventry fans rounded the corner. 'Let's fucking kill 'em!' they bellowed at their fellow Chelsea Firm members.

'It tastes funny,' Harry heard Hermione say in a muffled voice.

'Shit!' said Ron, as Harry died.

'There's something funny about Professor Hitler . . .' said Harry.

Hedwig was to be the last owl culled in the wake of the Hogwarts bird-flu scare.

'George Galloway is our new master of the Dark Arts.'

Harry felt Professor Snape's hot breath on the back of his neck.

'This is better than chasing real dragons,' said Harry, as he took the tin foil and rolled-up tenner.

'*Overus Actus!*' said Hermione.

And that, children, is why reading is bad for you.

That weird, thumping sound from the Forbidden Forest was the sound of a dead horse being flogged.

'Quick, if we use our broomsticks to fly to the top of the Tree of Enlightenment, we'll be able to see Hermione having a shower.'

'Do you realise we'll be thirty when they make the film of this one?' said Ron glumly.

The audience gasped as Harry got his cock out and blinded a horse.

Harry Potter had won – the evil witch JK Rowling would never write again.

UNLIKELY MEDICAL LABELS

DOSAGE: 42 IF SUICIDE DESIRED.

MAY CAUSE UNCONSCIOUSNESS
IN THAT GIRL YOU FANCY AT THE BAR,
BUT YOU DIDN'T HEAR IT FROM US, OK?

MAY CAUSE DIARRHOEA, DYSENTERY,
FLATULENCE, PILES AND OTHER HILARIOUS
BOTTOM-RELATED AILMENTS.

DO NOT ATTEMPT TO PICK ON SOMEONE BIGGER
AND TOUGHER THAN YOU.

WARNING: MAY LEAD TO GROWING
AN EXTRA LIMB OR, IN EXTREME CASES,
TWO HEADS.

SHOULD NOT BE TAKEN IRONICALLY.

MAY KILL OR CAUSE YOU TO KILL OTHERS.

DO NOT GIVE TO CHILDREN
UNLESS THEY ARE REALLY PISSING YOU OFF.

DO NOT TAKE IF BREATHING.

MAY CAUSE HOMOSEXUALITY.

DO NOT ADMIT TO TAKING
IF TRYING TO IMPRESS SOMEONE.

SWALLOW PILL, COUNT TO TEN,
BREATHE OUT, FINGERS CROSSED.

DO NOT BECOME ADDICTED TO
. . . OOPS, TOO LATE.

KEEP AWAY FROM SMALL CHILDREN,
YOU PAEDO.

DO NOT STOP THINKING ABOUT TOMORROW.

STORE IN A COOL, DRY PLACE
IF YOU KNOW OF ANYWHERE, WHICH I DOUBT.

CHILDREN: 1 TABLET DAILY
ADULTS: 3 TABLETS DAILY
AMY WINEHOUSE: 34 TABLETS IMMEDIATELY.

WARNING: DON'T SAY WE DIDN'T WARN YOU.

IF YOU HAVE BEEN PRESCRIBED THESE,
IT'S PROBABLY ALREADY TOO LATE.

SMEAR ONTO TESTICLES,
NOT NECESSARILY YOUR OWN.

WARNING: HAS NO EFFECT OTHER THAN
MAKING YOU THINK SOMETHING IS HELPING IN
THE LAST FEW, MISERABLE DAYS OF
YOUR EXISTENCE.

FOR BEST RESULTS, TAKE WHEN NOT ILL.

IMPROBABLE TV LISTINGS

Saturday 14th

9.00 a.m. Long Way Down
Finally, Ewan McGregor and Charley Boorman drive themselves and their fucking motorbikes off the top of Canary Wharf.

9.30 a.m. The Friday Night Project
Guest host Osama bin Laden joins Alan and Justin for knockabout fun and games.

11.00 a.m. Escape to the Country
A convicted sex offender on the run is looking for a remote Scottish croft all but inaccessible from the mainland.

12.00 p.m. Loose Women
This week the panel take it in turns to fellate a screeching Dean Gaffney and a sweating Freddie Starr.

12.30 p.m. All-Star Family Fortunes
Former Nottingham Forest midfielder Ian Woan's family take on the man who used to play Winston in *Eastenders* and his relatives. Vernon Kay hosts.

1.00 p.m. Animal Park
Ben Fogle and Kate Humble shoot and skin tigers at Longleat. [Repeat]

2.00 p.m. The Tudors
After emailing a greeting to the King of Spain, Henry helicopters himself to the 'Field of Cloth and Gold'.

3.00 p.m. Celebrities in Need
Terry Wogan is your reasonably priced host as a wealth of celebrities remind you of their talents and availability including: BBC Newsreaders pitching for light-entertainment work; the cast of *Eastenders* doing songs from the shows to help raise vital versatility on their showreels; a lazy version of an ailing panel-show format with celebrities too dull to do the actual show; and three hours of songs from the casts of West End shows with box office details on the screen throughout.

6.00 p.m. The 100 Greatest Things that Haven't Been in One of These Lists Already
Jimmy Carr presents.

6.30 p.m. Who Do You Think You Are?
Sir Patrick Moore explains that he is now convinced he is a fieldmouse in a story by Beatrix Potter.

7.30 p.m. FILM: Police Academy 34: Mission to Stockwell
Commissioner Blair lets the bungling cadets tackle a fleeing suspected suicide bomber at a London Underground station, with catastrophic consequences.

9.00 p.m. Heartbeat
A mysterious stranger arrives in Aidensfield and either commits a crime or causes an accident. Featuring music that always makes you say, 'I didn't think this was from the Sixties.'

10.00 p.m. Time Team
Tony Robinson and the gang investigate some mysterious skeletons found in Rillington Place, London.

10.30 p.m. Bloodiest Ever You've Been Framed
Hilarious tea-time round-up of snuff movies, Jihadi calls to arms and underage pornography sent in by viewers.

11.00 p.m. Match of the Day
Thanks to satellite TV kick-offs, extended fifty-minute highlights of the only game of the day: Hull City versus Wigan Athletic. Messrs Lineker, Hansen and Shearer try to sound interested.

11.50 p.m. CSI Orkneys
Whilst investigating a child sex ring on a Sunday, Detective Brodie finds himself locked in a giant wicker effigy.

1.30 a.m. An Audience with Nick Griffin
Near-the-knuckle humour from the BNP funnyman, as an all-white celebrity audience joins in the japes.

2.00 a.m. Countdown
98% of people who die do so during this programme.

2.30 a.m. The X Factor
The results of next week's phone votes.

3.00 a.m. Icons of the Seventies
Gary Glitter talks to Jonathan King . . . oh, someone really should have checked the tape before putting this out . . .

3.30 a.m. Question Time
This week, David Dimbleby is pushing his own agenda in Winchester.

4.30 a.m. Rick Stein's Mediterranean Escapes
The popular chef tunnels out of a Turkish prison with a homicidal drag queen.

5.00 a.m. Chris Langham in the Psychiatrist's Chair
Episode 2 of 607.

6.00 a.m. Who Do You Think You're Looking At?
Each week a celebrity goes into an East End pub, stares at people, spills pints and orders 'poofy drinks'.

BAD THINGS TO HEAR ON WAKING UP

'You'll never find your penis where I threw it.'

'This is Radio 1 and you're listening to the Chris Moyles Breakfast Show . . .'

'Would you mind awfully taking my cock out of your mouth now?'

'Welcome to Broadmoor, Sexy.'

'Shit! He's coming round, pull his trousers up for me.'

'Earth to earth, ashes to ashes, dust to dust . . .'

'Now we do have something in common: chlamydia.'

'You've wet the bed again, Prime Minister.'

'Is this your car, sir?'

'What are you doing in the gorilla enclosure?'

'Dad, that was amazing.'

'We meet at last, Mr Bond.'

'Where has your house gone?'

'Eurrgh, who's that in your bed?'

'Shit, he's waking up, nurse! Stop pissing about with his heart and I'll put it back in.'

'No, sorry, it wasn't a dream.'

'So, have I turned you gay then?'

'He's taken sixty now without bleeding.'

'There is some bad news about your good kidney . . .'

UNLIKELY THINGS TO FIND WRITTEN ON TOILET PAPER PACKAGING

WIPE BOTTOM, DROP INTO TOILET, FLUSH, REPEAT

NEW EXTRA STRONG FOR THOSE FRENZIED TEENAGE WANKS

NEW SANDPAPER SOFTNESS

NEW 4-PLY FOR THOSE TINY LITTLE ONES THAT
SMEAR OUT OF ALL CONTROL

BUY TWO SHITAWAYS, GET ONE SNOTAWAY FREE

LOW FAT

HOWEVER BEAUTIFUL SHE MIGHT BE, SHE'LL STILL USE THIS.
GET LADY LAV FOR THE WOMAN IN YOUR LIFE

NEW PARENTAL CONTROL TOILET PAPER,
WITH SEMEN-ACTIVATED ALARM SYSTEM

ANDREX BROWN FOR THE REALLY STUBBORN STAINS

JUST ADD GRAVY

NEW GILLIAN MCKEITH LOO ROLL,
ASSESSES YOUR DIET AS YOU WIPE

NEW SAT LAV – WOMAN'S VOICE
DIRECTS TO BITS YOU MAY HAVE MISSED

FLYPAPER LOO, AN END TO STICKY CLAGNUTS FOREVER

MAN RAG – FOR THE ARSEHOLE IN YOUR LIFE

NEW TWO-WAY WAX N' WIPE,
CLEANS YOUR BOTTOM AND SHAVES YOUR SACK AND CRACK

WITH NEW FRAGRANCE: SHIT

COMPUTER GAMES THAT WOULDN'T SELL

ACCORDIAN HERO 2

GARETH BATTY CRICKET

TRUE CRIME: STREETS OF CHIPPING SODBURY

CHARLES MANSON'S KILLING SPREE – RATED 12

GUITAR SADDO 3

WII FUCK

GRAND FRAUD ELECTORAL 4

ALAN TITCHMARSH GARDEN MASTER

STREET CLEANER II

WORLD OF HANDICRAFT

BORIS GOES CYCLING

SUPER MARIO BROS VS
HM INLAND REVENUE AND CUSTOMS

BANG BANG YAWN YAWN

VIRTUA TOWN PLANNER

PRO-EVOLUTION CREATIONIST

HAVE YOU BEEN OUTSIDE TODAY?

SELF ASSESSMENT TAX 8

UNLIKELY PUB NAMES

The Cock & Flasher

The Cat & Dysentery

The Donor & Liver

The Ominous Silence

The Inbred Locals

The Failing Marriage

The Rough & Racist

The Complexion & Rosacea

The Queen's C*nt

The Back, Sack & Crack

The Snot & Bacon

The Cannon & Ball

The Charles Kennedy

The Paralytic & Comatose

The Shock & Awe

The Blocked Toilet

The Ring o'Paedophiles

The Foot & Mouth

The Scratch & Sniff

The Leaky Scrotum

The Withered Arms

UNLIKELY MEDICAL LABELS

WARNING: IF YOU'RE STILL ALIVE AFTER
FIVE MINUTES, YOU'LL BE FINE.

INSERT PENIS HERE.

TRY OPERATING HEAVY MACHINERY
FOR A LAUGH.

MAY CAUSE FUNNY JOKES ABOUT THE NEWS
IF TAKEN TOPICALLY.

WARNING: TASTES AWFUL BUT THAT'S
THE LEAST OF YOUR TROUBLES, PAL, DO YOU
WANT BOILED SWEETS OR TO STOP THE
UNBEARABLE FUCKING PAIN?
YOUR CHOICE.

MAY CAUSE DEATH.

CRUSH UP AND SMOKE IN PIPE.

AS NOT TESTED ON ANYONE SO FAR.

RUB ON GUMS OR INGEST NASALLY, PREFERABLY
FROM THE BUTTOCKS OF
A CALL GIRL.

NO RABBITS WERE HARMED DURING THE
TESTING OF THIS PRODUCT – BUT THE RATS
WERE LESS LUCKY.

INSERT ANALLY TEN TIMES AN HOUR.

NOT QUITE READY YET.

SIDE-EFFECTS: MAY CAUSE LONG
UNINTERRUPTED ERECTION IF YOU'RE LUCKY.

WARNING: DID YOU SEE WHAT HAPPENED TO
THE SIX STUDENTS WE TESTED THIS ON?
NO? GOOD.

MAY LEAD TO BAD LANGUAGE AND SCENES OF A
SEXUAL NATURE FROM THE OUTSET.

MAY CAUSE YOU TO PLAY THE PIANO.

DO NOT TAKE IF PLANNING TO GO OUT AND GET
C*NTED.

INSERT THREE FEET UP RECTUM – YOU MAY
NEED TO BORROW A FRIEND'S FOOT.

DO NOT TAKE.

DISCARDED ADVERTISING SLOGANS

And all because
the lady's taken out a restraining order

Because you're worthless

Say goodbye to persistent foot pain
with this chainsaw

Plop plop fizz fizz
– the sound from Amy Winehouse's toilet

Maybe she's born with it, maybe it's a wig?

The milk chocolate that melts in your pocket,
not in your hand

Milky Way
– The sweet you can eat between meals
if you really don't have any willpower,
you greedy bastard

Go to work on an E

No FT, not really a problem

Happiness is a pipe called crack

Fastbuck Homes,
building boxes on flood plains since 1997

Your fragrance, your fault

Where do you want to go today?
Well tough, you're going to be sat at your desk
in front of your Microsoft computer, again
You'll wonder where the yellow went
when you brush with Eraserdent.
Come to that, you'll wonder where
your teeth went

The best a man can get for a paltry amount

The future's bright if you don't live on Earth

Come to sunny Marlboro Country
– which may lead to lung cancer

The man from Del Monte, he says,
'I'm sure I can be persuaded somehow,
you big strapping farmer you'

New diet drink will help you lose weight
– you'll get cancer from all the sweetener

Consolidate all your debts with us
– and your house will be ours in a year

REJECTED FIRST LINES OF GREAT POEMS

In Xanadu did Kubla Khan
A branch of Tesco's once decree.

Seasons of mists and mellow fruitfulness
Leaves on the line and sudden cancellations.

I wandered lonely through the crowd
Stealing credit cards and dollar bills.

O my love is like a red, red cock, newly sprung at dawn.

If you can keep your head when all about you are speaking
Arabic into a video camera . . .

The Owl and the Pussycat went to sea, only one came back.

Shall I compare thee to a summer's day?
Thou art as wet and disappointing, the trains are late, actually,
I say it's wet but with the bloody hosepipe ban . . .

Tyger, tyger burning bright
On my barbecue Tuesday night.

I met a traveller from an antique land who said,
'How I get British passport?'

They went to sea in a sieve, they did, in a sieve, the silly c*nts.

Half a league, half a league,
Between Man U and Liverpool these days.

O Wild West Wind, thou breath of Autumn's being,
Please blow up that woman's skirt.

In Xanadu did Mandelson
A useless fucking Dome decree.

My heart aches and a drowsy numbness pains all down my
arms, fuck I'm having a stroke!

How do I love thee? Let me count the ways . . .
Missionary, doggy and anal: three.

No man is an island, unless you count the Isle of Man.

Fifteen men on a dead man's chest,
Filming him on their phones.

It is the England goalkeeper
And he stoppeth one of three.

The Sea is calm tonight, but I'm shitting my pants.

'Twas the night before Christmas, when all through the house,
Burglars took everything, even my spouse.

HYMNS THE CHURCH PREFERS TO FORGET

'How Great Thou Arse'

'Christ on a Bike'

'It Was the Jews What Done It'

'Four and Twenty Virgins'

'While Shepherds Flashed their Cocks One Night'

'If You're Catholic and You Know It'

'Burn the Heretics, Hear the Scream'

'Don't Use a Johnny'

'In a Faraway Field, I was Shagged by the Priest'

'One John the Baptist, There's Only . . .'

'That was Amazing, Grace!'

'I was Cold, I was Naked, Which I Know isn't
an Excuse but . . .'

'Good King Wenceslas Came Out and Wed a Bloke
Called Stephen'

'Abide With Me, Lord, It Would Really Help with the Mortgage'

'Once in Royal Tunbridge Wells'

'There's Holly and there's Ivy, You Should Hear Them Groan'

BAD THINGS TO SAY AT A WEDDING

'If the bride would raise her veil, I will invite the groom to kiss the . . . whoa, Jesus, rather you than me, son.'

'Now a photo of the bridesmaids . . . lovely . . . if you can just lose your tops.'

'Paul has met a beautiful woman, someone he gets on with, who shares his interests and loves him as much as he loves her, but he realised last night that he had to forget about her and get on with the business of marrying Sandra.'

'Wow. You are wearing white. I thought it was a joke.'

'I've known the groom for twelve years. We met in a club in London and had a passionate one night stand before deciding we worked better as friends.'

'Rashid is delighted to be marrying Linda and getting a British passport, but obviously more the marrying Linda bit.'

'May I offer a roast to the bridesmaids, sorry, toast.'

'If anyone here knows of any just cause or impediment . . . bloody hell, form a queue, let's do this one at a time.'

'Please don't throw confetti – or bottles.'

'Can I just say how lovely the mother of the bride looks . . . when she's about to come.'

'They are a well-matched couple with great intelligence – believe me, I just ran my eyes over the pre-nup, and it's watertight.'

UNLIKELY US IMMIGRATION CARD QUESTIONS

1. Have you recently concealed any illegal drugs up your ass?

2. Are you a terrorist intent on causing mass destruction in the city you are visiting? If YES, please provide details.

3. List your five favorite Michelle Obama outfits.

4. Are you bringing in goods or currency exceeding a value of $1,000,000? If so, leave it in a bag in Central Park, no questions asked or the girl gets it.

5. Is that a UK passport in your pocket or are you just pleased to see me?

6. Do you like me? Are these questions too easy?

7. Have you now or at any time walked on soil? Please give a detailed description of each occasion.

8. Are you a fugitive Nazi war criminal? (A YES will not affect your chances of entering the country.)

9. Which of the cast of *Friends* would you do first?

10. If you are on a short stay, please give details of hotel and possibly places to eat, bars, shows, tourist destinations and lively nightspots.

11. Is this the card you were thinking of?

12. Are you traveling with any members of your family?
    If NO, what are you doing tonight?

13. In your hand luggage do you have any agricultural machinery such as a combine harvester or threshing machine?

14. What is your star sign?

15. Are you or have you ever been Cat Stevens?

16. Is your job something you do outdoors? Could I do it?
    Do you wear a uniform? Do you serve the public?
    Am I getting warm?

17. Are you smuggling in a pig or is that yo mama?

18. Are you here on business, pleasure, or making a sneery, self-indulgent documentary for BBC4?

19. Have you ever taken part in genocide? If NO, how many people have you killed:
    a) 1–10
    b) 10–100
    c) lost count but not genocide
    d) yeah, OK then, it was genocide
    If d), did they deserve it?

DISCARDED ADVERTISING SLOGANS

Curry sauce-flavoured condoms
– for when you pull a biffa

BP – it might look like a flower,
but it's still fucking petrol

To be honest, one razor blade is quite enough

We at Sainsbury's say 'Try something new today'.
Like shopping at Tesco!

There are a lot of sexy girls in this advert,
but to be honest, all lager tastes the same

Cadbury's Flake
– you're meant to think it's a cock

How hairy are your testicles?

Despite the lilting Irish voiceover, never forget:
it's only cider

WAP-based protocol, internet applications
and Bluetooth connectivity . . . are just three things
you'll never use on this overpriced phone

New tampons – Run, swim, eat chocolate,
bite your husband's head off

Condoms – ribbed inside and out.
Why should she have all the fun?

This is a classy and very funny ad
– but you'll never remember what it's for

This is our logo – to be honest,
we're as disappointed as you are

Poison – It does exactly what it says on the tin

We say our pasta sauce is made in the EU
to conjure up images of sun-baked Italian fields,
rather than the grey industrial sheds in Holland
where it's actually made

British Airways, the world's favourite airline.
If the company's paying

Take two bottles into the shower?
You've got two hands, why not?

You can buy this car if you like,
but you'll never go this fast yourself

ILL-ADVISED FIRST LINES OF BIOGRAPHIES

'Nothing interesting ever happens to me.'

'My name is Ann Widdecombe and I'm going to talk to you about my sex life.'

'It's not easy being Alan Titchmarsh's brother.'

'Andreas Pankarisos is my real name, but you know me as Andy Pandy.'

'But that's enough about me.'

'Let's begin at the beginning: first a swirling cloud of cosmic gas cooled to form what we call the Sun . . .'

'You will like this autobiography, but not a lot.'

'I hope you won't find my life as boring as I have.'

'This is all about my lifelong struggle with amnesia.'

'Speaking as a mayfly . . .'

'Now, child-killers don't always get a good press . . .'

'I vividly recall the time
It first occurred to me to rhyme . . .'

'I was named Cliff Richard but not *the* Cliff Richard.'

'People always ask me how I first came up with the idea for the paper-clip.'

'I always were and always would be a terrible writerer.'

'Colonic irrigation has always fascinated me, as this 'scratch 'n' sniff' autobiography illustrates.'

'I was inspired to write by Salman Rushdie's brilliant *Satanic Verses.*'

'I suppose most people know me as Private Sponge from *Dad's Army*, but this is the story of the real Colin Bean.'

'It's always been tough being a narcoleptic and zzzzzzzzzzzzzzzzz.'

'They call me the World's Most Irritating Man. How unfair. Hear ye, history will judge me differently after this . . . read on, McDuff! (I know it should be 'Lead on' but this is a joke and don't worry, it isn't the last . . .).'

'The first thing I should tell you is that I'm not really blind and Sadie is just a pet.'

'OK, so my sisters moved to England, had a hit and one dated a politician, but what about the brother they left behind in Romania – the Cheeky Boy?'

UNLIKELY EMAILS TO FIND IN YOUR INBOX

We are doing a survey to see how alike people's bank details are. Please send us yours. We are honest. Honest.

I'm a Nigerian general – just wondering how things are with you?

Hi, I'm a really sexy and cool woman of your dreams and I spend all my time logged in to Internet dating sites as well.

Is your erection functioning perfectly?

Hello, son, it's your mum here, I've just uploaded some JPEGs onto your zipdrive, I'll try and import some Firefox cookies over to your hard drive a bit later on . . .

No milk today, please.

Reply all: Will you marry me? Yes/no/can I get back to you [delete as appropriate].

Titslutjizzbucket16 would like to offer you a new low-interest credit card.

Hi. I don't know how to use email.

Xvtruc%987234.99.xcernm.99v says, 'Hi Mate. How are you? Long time no see.'

Hey Big Boy, it's Katy. Are we still having our torrid affair on Wednesdays when my husband Ian is at football training? Just let me know. Love, Katy. (Not Ian, definitely not.)

BAD THINGS TO SAY AT A WEDDING

'Let's have one of the bride flashing her garter . . . now one with her knickers on.'

'The next hymn was chosen by the bride, although it's clearly not about her – "All Things Bright and Beautiful".'

'If we could dim the lights, I will now spend twenty minutes trying and failing to set up an anticlimactic slide and PowerPoint show . . .'

'When you throw rice, you're meant to take it out of the bag.'

'Till WHAT us do part?'

'You may kiss the bride, she love you long time.'

'We've done the other group photos – now for everybody who's slept with the bride.'

'Till death or a canoe fraud do us part.'

'Which one of you has the cock rings?'

'We've done an exclusive for the photos – with Razzle magazine.'

'I've been asked not to talk about the stag do, not by the groom, but by the embarrassed teenage boy he shagged.'

'If anyone knows any reason why they should not be wed – well, I'll start the ball rolling.'

'Go on – if I shag you, I'll have done the full set of bridesmaids.'

'I've never seen a bride looking as lovely as Jennifer does today – and believe me, I've seen some pretty strong contenders on hotbrides-beggingforaction.com.'

'Since you ask, this isn't the first time I've met your sister.'

UNFORTUNATE NAMES FOR RACE HORSES

I'M WELL HUNG

HEAD IN THE BED

FRENCH LUNCH

UNDERAGE SEX

RUG MUNCHER

FUCKED UP THE ARSE

IT HURTS WHEN I PEE

OBVIOUSLY ON DRUGS

SUCK MY COCK

STRANGELY ATTRACTIVE

MENGELE'S MISCHIEF

COME ON YOU C*NT!

I'M LEAVING YOU, YOU BITCH

UNSIGHTLY RASH

RUSSIAN ANUS

JAILBAIT

PRITT STICK

SHITS WHERE IT LIKES

SMOTHERED THE TWINS

ELECTRODES TO THE GONADS

PHILIP'S A RACIST

JANETTE KRANKIE'S MINGE

STICKY DISCHARGE

PETER SUTCLIFFE'S DELIGHT

CAT MEAT

UNLIKELY CROSSWORD CLUES

ACROSS

1. Hooray for the Gunners – sorry love, I changed lanes by accident – the ascent of Gary Glitter (2, 3, 4)

8. Things that my dick has been said to be (4)

9. Rip van Winkle's name (3, 3, 6)

10. Wife berates recalcitrant husband 'You f_____ c_____!' (7, 4)

11. Columnist on this newspaper that no one likes (6, 8)

12. My wife's nickname for my penis (7)

15. Something that will get you a fatwa (6, 8, 7)

16. Are you a paedo? (3)

17. Guess my name or I can have your first-born daughter (15)

20. Irritating fucking Japanese numbers game that everyone prefers to crosswords now (2, 4)

21. Your innermost secret (fill in the whole grid and send in)

22. BlahblahohwhatsthepointIvebeendoingthistoolong

DISCARDED ADVERTISING SLOGANS

Own-brand sausages – who'd have thought
an arsehole could taste so good?

Just because I'm wearing overalls and a badge saying
'Can I help you?', it doesn't mean I can help you

Exclusively with the Daily Mail, a fantastic free DVD
– of a long-forgotten American mini-series
that everyone hated at the time

Kills 99% of all known germs
– leaving the deadly 1% still alive

Buy a 4x4 and stuff the planet
– cos the kids shouldn't have to walk
a hundred yards to school

For mash, get potatoes

Ladyshave
– The best a clam can get

Special-strength lager
– enjoy it in your favourite park or alleyway

Cadbury's Creme Eggs
– How do you regurgitate yours?

'Mummy, why are your hands so soft?'
'Because that nice Bulgarian girl does the washing up'

Tired of the same old porn?

It's not just Haemorrhoid cream,
it's lip gloss too!

Take two rent boys into the shower?

How many times have you thought,
'I wish I hadn't shagged that goat?'

Hi, I'm the President of Iran,
and I liked Russian Uranium so much
that I bought the company

Hi, I'm Robert Mugabe, and I'm here to talk to you
about indigestion relief

This beautiful sofa looks lovely, doesn't it?
But it won't look half as good in your
cramped front room

Our new ultra-high-fibre bran cereal
will go through without touching the sides!

Budgetair – We're the cheapest,
because we don't give a shit about you or anything

THINGS YOU NEVER HEAR
ON THE RADIO

'You're listening to 6-0-6, two hours of whining about referees . . .'

'My telly career never took off because I'm plug ugly.'

'And as you can hear, the black ball is right against the cushion, behind three reds.'

'And now, another patronising edition of *Woman's Hour*.'

'This is Capital Radio and that's enough adverts – now, back to the adverts.'

'Attention all shipping – buy a radar, this isn't the 1930s.'

'Now Paul Merton, let's have "just a minute" on the joy of fisting.'

'For those of you at home, the Archbishop of Canterbury is wearing a gimp mask.'

'And now here's that ugly bird with the travel.'

'Good evening and welcome to the Bridlington Mime Festival . . .'

'This is Radio 3, and if you're both listening I'll put on that Beethoven CD.'

'And as you join us here at Lord's, the batsman's holding the bowler's wil– oh sod it, they're just having gay sex.'

'Here's some travel advice: if you want to get anywhere, buy a helicopter.'

'Hi, you're listening to Mike Reid – the one that didn't die.'

'And now *The Archers*, and Old Seth has just been caught cottaging in Ambridge High Street . . .'

'So it's 4 a.m. listeners, and I'm the only thing between you and suicide.'

'And new in at number one, having sold sixteen copies, it's . . .'

'Before we close on Radio 4, it's time for A Wank at Bedtime.'

'And you've gone for an unusual desert island luxury . . . six hookers and a wrap of crack.'

UNFORTUNATE NAMES FOR RACE HORSES

MISOGYNIST COMMENT

PREMATURE EJACULATION

PUBE IN THE SOAP

KIDDY FIDDLER

YOUR FACE MY ARSE

JEFFREY DAHMER'S FRIDGE

GOLLIWOG

BALLSFUCKC*NTSHITWANKTITS

DWARF IN THE SADDLE

ONE UP THE BUM

I'VE PUT A FORTUNE ON THIS BASTARD

STRANGLED AT BIRTH

DANIEL RADCLIFFE'S COCK

OUR LITTLE SECRET

MY WIFE'S FRIGID

I'M IN THE CLOSET

WILL BE SHOT

UNPROTECTED SEX

EDWARD'S A POOF

STUMPY

GARY GLITTER'S WEAKNESS

JOCKEY FUCKER

TRIPOD

SCHINDLER'S LIST

REJECTED SLOGANS FOR THE
LONDON OLYMPICS

LONDON 2012: WAY OVER BUDGET

WE'RE NOT FAR FROM PARIS

LET'S HOPE WE DON'T GET BOMBED

SORRY ABOUT THE TRANSPORT

COULD BE WORSE, YOU COULD BE IN MANCHESTER

WHO CARES?

COME FOR THE OLYMPICS, STAY FOR ASYLUM

LARGELY STEROID FREE

AT LEAST WE'LL WIN THE ROWING

WE'RE TAKING THE URINE

LONDON 2013. BETTER LATE THAN NEVER

HIGHER, FURTHER, FASTER, MORE EXPENSIVE

*IS THAT A STARTER'S PISTOL IN YOUR POCKET,
OR ARE YOU MUGGING ME?*

*HACKNEY MARSHES – A SOLID FOUNDATION FOR
THE OLYMPICS*

UK GOLD – STILL JUST A TV CHANNEL

UNLIKELY US IMMIGRATION CARD QUESTIONS

1. How much bigger and stronger than your country is America?

2. Are you here on:
   a) business
   b) holiday
   c) working holiday
   d) a trip where you are meant to be working where it's more like a holiday
   e) a holiday where you may as well be in work you're getting that many phone calls,

   or

   f) jihad?

3. Were you ever a member of the Communist party? Have you met Brezhnev? If YES, what was he like?

4. Who was the best Dr Who?

5. Where were you on September 11, 2001? Give details. (If answer includes the phrase: 'Trying to board a plane with weapons and a copy of the Koran,' please go directly to Question 7.)

6. Would you ever wear brown shoes with black trousers?

7. Please list all US states in order of GDP. (Use additional sheet.)

8. How was your flight? What did you have for your tea?

9. Do you know where Amelia Earhart is?

10. Are you part of the Axis of Evil?

11. Can you read this out loud? I just love your accent.

12. How do you pronounce the word aluminum? Your entry depends on this.

13. Are you from England? Do you know my friend John? He lives there.

14. Did you kill Trotsky?

15. Only recently can US foreign policy be said to have stepped out of the shadow cast by the Vietnam war. Discuss.

16. Are you looking at my girlfriend?

17. Complete this sentence in ten words or less: 'I have always wanted to visit America because . . .'

18. When did you last use the toilet? Well, why didn't you go before you left?

19. Please fill in this card with stickers of US presidents. We've started you off with a free Bill Clinton, Gerald Ford and Grover Cleveland.

20. Have you recently visited Canada? Shit, isn't it?

DISCARDED ADVERTISING SLOGANS

Do people laugh at your penis?

Pampers nappies – we're full of shit

Have you got a clean licence and five years' no claims bonus?
Then you'll get a good deal from anybody,
you certainly don't need us

Treat yourself to a Duchy Original biscuit
– all profits go towards curing my wife's distemper

Dropping the kids off at the ex-wife's?
Then pack 'em full of lemonade and buy them a drum kit

This exciting new five-litre sports car
– will get you banned in 4.6 seconds

Are you starting to get wrinkles?
Well, you're bound to at your age

The best a man can get is twin sisters and a gram of cocaine.
Sod shaving

Drink our spring water – filtered through rock for
thousands of years. Best before November

Chocolate Orange: tap it, unwrap it, make yourself sick

Today in your Super Soaraway Sun:
read some made-up bollocks about a shark
then have a crafty wank over Page 3

LIES FROM EVERYDAY LIFE

'There is a good service on all London Underground lines.'

'No, it wasn't me, it must have been the dog.'

'Yes, your penis is bigger than my previous boyfriend's.'

'You'll get it tomorrow, I sent it first class.'

'Your call is very important to us.'

'This summer's must have.'

'You've had a facelift? I never would have known.'

'Of course it doesn't put me off, Heather.'

'I'm not a racist but . . .'

'A watched pot never boils.'

'No thanks, I've already bought a *Big Issue* this week.'

'It's my glands.'

'Your minicab will be with you in two minutes.'

'Oh was she not wearing a bra? I didn't notice.'

'I've no idea how that site got onto my Internet "history".
Must be a virus.'

PUBLIC TRANSPORT ANNOUNCEMENTS YOU'LL NEVER HEAR

'As we pull out of Bristol Temple Meads, I'd like to read to you from my as yet unpublished novel.'

'As the weather is so hot, we will switch on the air conditioning.'

'These tickets are real value for money.'

'And just behind the buffet car is the jacuzzi.'

'I never feel safer than when I'm in an empty carriage in the middle of the night, near Reading.'

'If you're an attractive young woman, you may want to make your way to Carriage C, where a highly respected judge will be exposing his penis.'

'We're getting there, but really slowly.'

'If you look out the window, you will see the same thing you saw two hours ago.'

'I wonder what the age of this train really is?'

'For those of you unable to read screens, boards, the front of trains or believe any of the passengers around you, the train you have just seemingly taken a punt on boarding is going to Southampton.'

'Choose from one of 107 different fares.'

'The bar is now open for sandwiches, chocolate and scalding-hot water.'

'Get your dicks ou . . . tickets, I meant tickets.'

'You're on the Penzance to Inverness, and this is James Blunt . . .'

'If you look down the toilets, you can see the track!'

'That little bobbly thing that you put your foot on to work the flush . . . will not work.'

'After I say "go", the first person to pull the emergency cord wins £10.'

'You will need to take a rail replacement coach all the way, so we will happily charge you less for the journey.'

'Coach E is for any single people who might like to size up the talent.'

'Owing to a fatality at Clapham Junction, this train is currently driverless and heading into the buffers at East Croydon at 167 miles an hour.'

'If you're interested in seeing some history during your journey, can I draw your attention to the toilets in Coach F; they haven't been flushed since 1988 and contain some of the finest fossilized stools in the country.'

LIES FROM EVERYDAY LIFE

'Thank you, Granny, that was delicious.'

'Socks – just what I wanted!'

'I'd love to come but we're away that weekend.'

'No, I really can't spare two minutes for your charity.'

'I just had the one quick drink after work,
but the traffic home was terrible.'

'You'll really go places with this media studies degree.'

'Remember, your vote counts.'

'There's a caller at the front door – I hope it's
that man selling overpriced j-cloths.'

'100% beef'.

'I'd happily stop flying to prevent global warming.'

'You've got to admire Richard Branson.'

'I love you, Lembit.'

'The Eden project – what a great day out.'

'We need a Range Rover in Surbiton.'

'It's not exams that have got easier;
children are just cleverer these days.'

'That Victoria Beckham, she's a looker isn't she?'

'That Nazi costume will go down a treat, Harry.'

'I did not see the penalty incident.'

'Your safety is our priority.'

'The only reason we have to finish is because
I love you too much.'

'To have and to hold, for better or worse,
for richer or poorer . . .'

'Sorry darling, it slipped up there by accident.'

'No darling, that fits beautifully.'

'The winner of the People's Choice Comedy Award is . . .
Ant and Dec!'

'The manager has our full support.'

LINES YOU WON'T FIND IN THE BIBLE

To be continued.

So Jesus made them all bacon sandwiches.

'I haven't got any swaddling I'm afraid,' said the Innkeeper, 'but there is this old romper suit.'

'Sorry, the myrrh got confiscated by customs.'

'You're bang out of order Pharaoh, do you know what I mean?' said Moses.

And on the eighth day he didn't do much because it was a Bank Holiday.

'Do that again Eve,' said Adam, 'but first lick your lips yeah?'

Jonah was swallowed by a giant fish and decided that now was the time to lay off LSD.

'I told you we should make a reservation,' shouted Mary, 'it's bloody Christmas.'

'Follow the star? Tonight? It's the final of X Factor.*'*

'Shit! There's a fucking lion in here!' said Daniel.

'How shall I build the Ark, Lord?' asked Noah. 'With this allen key,' said God.

'I'm telling Mum,' said Isaac.

'Best of three?' said Goliath's big brother as David wheeled away in triumph.

'There's three of us in this marriage,' said Joseph.

And lo, all the creatures of land and sea evolved gradually over millions of years.

And Abraham did beget Isaac and Isaac did beget Jacob, and Jacob was gay so that was the end of that.

Thou shalt take thy healing crystals, sit under a pyramid and chant 'Ommm'.

In the beginning was the word and the word was . . . 'contifabulation'. Sandy Toksvig goes first!

'Good news, Jesus,' said Pontius Pilate, 'I'm commuting your sentence to "life".'

Slowly, tenderly, Joseph's fingers inched up Mary's silken thigh.

And so the Messiah was born, on a day that would for ever be celebrated as . . . Winterval.

The wise men came from the East. And the foolish man came on Network South-East, and arrived on the 27th.

Everything I'm saying is good for two thousand years, until Richard Dawkins gets here.

Can you change it back to water again, mate? I'm driving.

I'm sure we had two of everything, Mrs Noah – not just two fat lions.

About the Author: God lives and works everywhere. He has one son. This is his first book.

Eternal life is not guaranteed and may depend on past performance; your soul may go down as well as up.

COMPETITIONS NO ONE WOULD ENTER

GET HUMPED BY A DOBERMAN-A-THON

WIN A FARM IN ZIMBABWE

GMTV'S LATEST PHONE VOTE

HOW MUCH ASBESTOS CAN YOU INHALE?

WIN A CHANCE TO JOIN THE DOTS ON DEAN GAFFNEY'S FACE

WHO'S GOT BRITAIN'S TINIEST COCK?

WIN A TREKKING HOLIDAY WITH JIMMY SAVILE

THE BAGHDAD MARATHON

STICK YOUR HAND IN THIS HOLE

AL-QAEDA 'PASS THE PARCEL'

THREE LUCKY *MIRROR* READERS CAN BE
CIRCUMCISED TOMORROW

AN ALL-EXPENSES-PAID TRIP TO KFC

STRICTLY CUM

SPOT THE BALL AND WIN A CHANCE
TO SERVE IN AFGHANISTAN FOR TWO WEEKS

YOUR CHANCE TO TAKE PART IN CHEMICAL TRIALS
FOR A NEW DRUG

MISS IRAN

A DRINKING CONTEST WITH CHARLES KENNEDY

ELEPHANT MAN LOOKALIKE COMPETITION

READER'S DIGEST PRIZE DRAW

WIN A THONG WORN BY PETER STRINGFELLOW

CLEANEST FRENCHMAN

SCOTLAND'S MEANEST MAN – ENTRY £1

WIN A TEN-MINUTE TROLLEY DASH AT LIDL

WIN A TWO-WEEK HOLIDAY FOR FIVE
IN DONCASTER

MEET THE STARS OF *HIGH SCHOOL MUSICAL*
(WELL, THE ONES WHO ARE OVER 30)

SIGN UP FOR THE NATIONAL DNA DATABASE AND WIN AN
ELECTRONIC ANKLE BRACELET

WIN TICKETS FOR A BEN ELTON MUSICAL

ROUND AUSTRALIA SWIMMING RACE

MR GAY ALABAMA

WIN A LUNCH DATE WITH VANESSA FELTZ

UNLIKELY CROSSWORD CLUES

DOWN

1. Cabinet minister and in-the-closet homosexual who tied me up and bummed me (6, 7)

7. Presenter of *Tonight with Jay Leno* (3,4)

8. Dyke, doughnut basher, rug muncher, bean flicker etc. (7)

9. My mum's maiden name (7)

10. One of the letters of the alphabet (1)

11. Who you should vote for in the next election (5, 7)

13. Type of 16th-century Dutch drinking vessel that only four people now living have heard of (7)

16. Not small – rhymes with pig (3)

17. Just fill in the blanks to look clever (9, 12)

20. Apricot knee Simon – well a nun might if the Zeppelin has grown its own Byzantium (16, 8)

21. Slang for female genital area or Russell Brand (4)

22. Greek god invented by crossword compilers (8)

DISCARDED HEADLINES FROM HISTORY

AS JESUS DIES, WE ASK 'WHERE'S YOUR TEARS, MARY?'

DIANA MARRIES CHARLES IN PARTNERSHIP
DOOMED TO END IN NASTY CAR ACCIDENT IN PARIS

ANOTHER RIPPER VICTIM! TO ADD TO YOUR
WALLCHART STICKER COLLECTION

ASTEROID STRIKE: MANY DINOSAURS DEAD

CATHERINE OF ARAGON: 'THERE ARE THREE OF US
IN THIS MARRIAGE'

FROGS, LOCUSTS, DARKNESS – IS CLIMATE CHANGE
RUINING EGYPT?

'FIRE WAS MY IDEA' CLAIM INVENTOR'S FRIENDS

'NOT IN OUR NAME' HUNS TAKE TO STREETS
TO PROTEST ATTILA'S INVASION OF GAUL

BUBONIC PLAGUE – AMERICAN LAB LIKELY SOURCE?

HENRY VIII – READ ABOUT MY BIRDS, THE BOOZE
AND THE BLOODBATHS, ONLY IN THIS SUNDAY'S
NEWS OF THE WORLD

BRITAIN DECLARES WAR ON GERMANY.
HOW WILL IT EFFECT HOUSE PRICES?

2966 WORLD CUP SPECIAL – CAN ENGLAND
END 1,000 YEARS OF HURT?

RAMESES CRITICISED OVER WEIRD POINTY TOMB THING

PAPER INVENTED – LOOK!

QUESTIONS OMITTED FROM THE DRIVING THEORY TEST

1. When cut up at the lights, what is the correct number of fingers to raise?

2. How long after the light turns red are you still allowed to go through it?

3. For how many days can a card saying 'Tax Applied For' be used?

4. Is it ever permissible to swerve into the nearside lane to splash an old lady?

5. True or false: the wing mirror on the passenger side is to see whether you knocked down that cyclist?

6. True or false: 'Bald tyres are sexy.'

7. 'Wee wee wee' or 'woo woo woo' – which of these distinctive car alarm noises will annoy your neighbours most?

8. You are joining a motorway while texting a friend and changing a CD. How do you eat your crisps?

9. In what circumstances can a home-made sign saying 'Doctor on Call' be used?

10. When was the last time you actually put gloves in your glove box?

11. You are taking a corpse to dump in a gravel pit. What is the best way to avoid that incriminating DNA evidence?

12. When leaving your car in a residential area late at night, how do you achieve maximum volume on a door slam?

13. You are driving a white van. Is there any law you need care about?

14. A cyclist is driving the wrong way up a one-way street. Are you allowed to hit him?

15. What the fuck is this?

16. If cut up by a white van is the correct response
    a) one finger
    b) two fingers
    c) 'wanker' gesture or d) terrified silence?

UNLIKELY FIRST LINES FOR LOVE SONGS

'You remind me of the M1.'

'I love you too much to let you live.'

'I don't mean any of this, I'm just angling for a shag.'

'I would shave my armpits for you.'

'You're the (next) best thing.'

'You took out your dentures.'

'It started with a fist . . .'

'Run your fingers through my back hair.'

'Tie me up and put an orange in my mouth.'

'Get your tits out for the lads.'

'You kept me in your basement until I was eighteen.'

'I've still got the herpes to remember you by.'

'Our death pact is strong.'

'I love you like the E4791 steam train from Newcastle.'

'I'll love you for the rest of your life . . . when the farmer takes you off to slaughter.'

'We met on the net and I ate you.'

UNLIKELY OBITUARIES

The world will be a sadder place without him, though not significantly.

He had a chequered career. Or, in other words, he was a crook.

Good riddance to the old c*nt.

This 'talentless, callow, backstabbing bastard', as he would like to be remembered.

She was a major screen star of the forties and was thought to be one of Britain's greatest beauties, but time wasn't kind to her, and by the time I shagged her, she was absolutely hideous.

Died suddenly and peacefully on an electric chair at the New York State Penitentiary.

The less said about him, the better.

The inventor of Cluedo, died in the conservatory, with a cardiac arrest.

He leaves a wife and four children, much as he did on several occasions during his life.

Some said he was unwise to criticize President Putin . . .

He leaves a wife, two children and absolutely fuck all to me, his supposed best friend.

He was a brash, flamboyant personality who didn't suffer fools gladly – a shit, in other words.

He has left a fortune of £100 million under his bed – finders keepers.

Born in 1873, he would have been 135, so that must be a mistake.

REJECTED NAMES FOR ROYAL NAVY SHIPS

HMS NANCY BOY

HMS SMITHEREENS

HMS PATRICIA ROUTLEDGE

HMS FRIENDLY FIRE

HMS CHLAMYDIA

HMS POSEIDON

HMS SKIMPED ON MATERIALS

HMS PEDALO

HMS AGROUND

HMS GIRL

HMS TOUCHY FEELY

HMS RECYCLABLE

HMS BUGGERY

HMS GLUG-GLUG-GLUG

HMS PHALLUS

HMS COMPROMISE

HMS TAMPON

HMS VULNERABLE

HMS BARBARA STREISAND

HMS RETARDED

HMS BUTTFUCK

HMS FLIMSY

HMS MACRAMÉ

HMS BAMBI

HMS L'ORÉAL

HMS ICEBERG

HMS PANIC

HMS DILDO

HMS NETBALL

HMS PORNOGRAPHIC

HMS PEA-GREEN BOAT

HMS JUMBLY

HMS LEAKING

HMS ROBINSON CRUSOE

HMS GRAHAM NORTON

HMS NOT A LOT OF LIFEBOATS, SORRY

HMS DROWNING

HMS SHIT-TIP

HMS CUTBACKS

HMS ABYSS

HMS SOMME

HMS ANUSOL

HMS COWARDICE

HMS LOVE BOAT

HMS FLOATING CEMETERY

HMS ECRET SERVICE

HMS COLANDER

HOW NOT TO END A NEWS BULLETIN

'I don't know why you're pretending to shuffle your papers, Bert.'

'And on a lighter note, Fluffy the cat today unearthed . . . a severed human head.'

'You couldn't make this shit up, could you?'

'On a personal note, I'm much too good for this.'

'And the missiles are on their way over to us as I speak . . . just kidding.'

'And the main points of the news again: blah blah blah.'

'And now, the end is near, and so I face the final curtain . . .'

'And now over to Susan for the weather . . . There's no whether about it, I definitely would.'

'Shit, that was my fucking street flooded there, everything will be ruined – my new carpet!'

'And in other news: my contract ends in a fortnight if you're watching, Sky.'

'That's it from a news bulletin that runs as smoothly as a Peugeot 307 from Ted Collins Motors of Lowestoft. They're great.'

'The Queen there, still pretty hot for 82, I think you'll agree.'

'It's goodnight from me and it's goodnight from him.'

UNLIKELY SMALL ADS

FOR SALE: Bloody hunting knife for sale. Make me an offer, quickly.

Half a cold latte for sale, only bought yesterday, would benefit from heating.

£20 – I wasn't born yesterday, but this baby was.

ERRATA: Thank you for the enquiries for the catamaran for sale for £10 yesterday, advert should have read: cat and meringue for sale, £10.

Gobstopper for sale, first three colours sucked off for you.

FOR SALE: litre of petrol, £10. Buyer collects.

Fancy a massage? I'm big and busty – with man boobs and a beer gut.

Pre-op transsexual – which I suppose translates as 'bloke'.

Animal lover and DIY enthusiast seeks to sell three-legged elephant plus umbrella stand.

Viagra wanted – unable to locate on the Internet anywhere.

Hitler diaries for sale. The perfect 2010 organizer for the Nazi in your life.

MUSICALS THAT DIDN'T MAKE IT TO BROADWAY

ALL THAT JIZZ

SEVEN BRIDES FOR SEVEN SISTERS

SEVEN ARRANGED MARRIAGES FOR
SEVEN BROTHERS

SEVEN BRIDES FOR SEVEN CHUCKLE BROTHERS

AN AMERICAN IN PARIS HILTON

GO WEST: THE FRED AND ROSE STORY

CORGI AND BESS:
THE STORY OF QUEEN ELIZABETH II
AND ONE OF HER DOGS

HEATHER MILLS IN . . . FOOTLOOSE

THE WOMAN IN WHITE, THE WOMAN IN BLACK,
FOR GOD'S SAKE, WOMAN, WE'VE GOT TO
BE THERE AT EIGHT

DOGS

WEARSIDE STORY

LES HAPPY

PIMP YOUR WAGON

ROOFER ON THE FIDDLE

PIRATE VIDEOS OF PENZANCE

GAYS AND DOLLS

RYVITA

CHITTY CHITTY GANG BANG

FRANK SINATRA AND GENE KELLY IN
ON THE PISS

PAINT YOUR WOGAN

JAILHOUSE COCK

THE SOUND OF MUCUS

JOSEPH AND HIS AMAZING AMOUNT OF
FREE PUBLICITY ON BBC 1 PRIMETIME

MEET ME IN ST HELENS

PAEDO OF THE OPERA

THE JOCKY WILSON PICTURE SHOW

ANNIE GET YOUR ASBO

GREASY

THOROUGHLY MODERN MILIBAND

UNLIKELY OBITUARIES

He leaves an enormous hole – in the left-hand side of his head.

A Tory minister, a high court judge, a military hero and regular churchgoer and now, I feel I can exclusively reveal . . . a paedophile.

. . . until he was killed by me.

It is fitting tribute that of the 5,000 people at her memorial service, she had shagged 4,900 of them.

For many years the voice of the speaking clock, his funeral will take place at 5.34 and 18 seconds precisely.

He will be missed, though not, ironically, by the Sudanese firing squad.

Accused of being a fugitive Nazi war criminal, something he vigorously denied all his life from his Argentine villa, 'Green Goebbels'. . .

He fought the march of time, valiantly but ultimately unsuccessfully. I mean, Christ, the hair plugs, the facelifts and the dyed eyebrows? Mickey Rooney has aged more gracefully.

He always felt 'twas not a crime, to handle his affairs in rhyme. The life he lived was not in vain, but he died in massive fucking pain.

It is said there are some people who are too good for this world, but Kenny certainly wasn't one of them.

He leaves a wife, two children and a bullet hole, along with a series of blood stains on his bedroom wall.

ILL-ADVISED NAMES FOR MILITARY OPERATIONS

OPERATION CLUELESS

OPERATION NO HOPE

OPERATION WASTE OF YOUNG LIFE

OPERATION QUAGMIRE

OPERATION CREAM PUFF

OPERATION HORRIFIC BLOODBATH

OPERATION DIDN'T THEY USED TO BE OUR FRIENDS?

OPERATION ILL-THOUGHT OUT

OPERATION CAN OF WORMS

OPERATION RUN LIKE FUCK

OPERATION DENGUE FEVER

OPERATION WE CAN BUT TRY

OPERATION DESSERT SPOON

OPERATION WHAT, IN THERE? AGAINST THEM?

OPERATION FUCKWITS

OPERATION LOOSE BOWELS

OPERATION GALLIPOLI

OPERATION LEMMING

OPERATION ONE THING AFTER ANOTHER

UNAPPETISING THINGS TO READ ON A MENU

Coq au man

Lightly toasted fillet of Jack Russell on a woodlouse celeriac

Testicles

The Not Really That Special

Board of cheeses
(Dairylea, Cheese Strings, Laughing Cow,
Primula and a selection of Wotsits)

Welcome to Gordon Banks at Claridge's

Weekly Specials:
Monday: *nothing*
Tuesday: *nothing*
Wednesday: *fuck all*
Thursday: *chef can't be arsed*
Friday: *an apple*
Saturday: *yeah right*
Sunday: *closed*

A 65% service charge will be added for your convenience
(We've added a further 20% to your bill as an added insult
on top of the dreadful service)

LINES YOU WON'T FIND IN THE BIBLE

And the Lord did summon to him as his followers James and his brother John, and Simon who is called 'Duckie'.

And the customers did return with their tables and chairs and said unto Jesus, 'This furniture is of shoddy quality.'

And lo, at the wedding feast the wine was all consumed and Jesus did take the jugs of water and spake unto his disciples, 'You'll like this, but not a lot.'

File under 'Fiction'.

And many Polish carpenters did appear in the land of Judea and did price the Lord out of business.

And Jesus did walk in the wilderness for forty days and forty nights before finally asking someone, 'Which aisle for household goods, please?'

Any resemblance to any characters dead or alive is purely coincidental.

If you take the first letter of every sentence in Genesis, it spells out 'The Da Vinci Code'.

Other religions are available.

Thou shalt not read out any bits on American television and ask for money.

And they all lived happily ever after. The End.

He who turns any part of this into a musical shall be cursed with a disfigured face.

TERRIBLE PICK-UP LINES

'I'm having it cut off tomorrow, so think of it as a sort of farewell voyage.'

'Would you like to see my penis?'

'That's just the psoriasis.'

'Come on, luv, I only need a Kraut for the full set.'

'So, how long have you been doing your own conveyancing?'

'Just stand slightly to the left, I'm trying to hide my stiffy.'

'It comes off at the knee, see?'

'Now are you definitely sixteen? Once bitten, twice shy and all that.'

'Hello. I'm Michael Winner.'

'Have you ever been to a Harvester before?'

'Do you mind inserting my enema?'

'You look ugly enough to be prepared to fuck me.'

'Mum, can I sleep in your bed tonight?

'My cock's on Myspace.'

'I'm Barry Scott, let's try a Cillit Bang.'

'Your sister was shit.'

'Would you like to see my puppetry of the anus?'

'How much for the whole night?'

'Hold me pint, I'm just going for a dump.'

'It's in there somewhere, have a good rummage, I know, it's like a needle in a bloody haystack.'

'Put this bag on your head will you, luv?'

'Well if I shag you and your dad, I've done all the family.'

'Have you got herpes as well?'

'You're even more beautiful than my cock.'

'What are your views on a European single currency?'

'How would you like to come home and squat over my coffee table?'

'You remind me of my daughter.'

'Oh sorry, is this the ladies'? Force of habit.'

'I felt sorry for you so thought I'd come over and say hello.'

'Oh go on, I've only got 48 hours to live.'

'Have you eaten? Well get your mouth round this.'

'Wrap me in your bingo wings.'

'You are either a beautiful man or a really ugly woman . . .'

THEATRE REVIEWS YOU'LL NEVER SEE

'THIS IS A LOAD OF SHIT.'

'VANESSA FELTZ IS PURE THEATRICAL VIAGRA.'

'MUG SOMEONE FOR A TICKET – NOW – STAB THEM
. . . HIM THERE, HE'LL DO . . .'

'DARREN DAY *IS* KING LEAR.'

'YOU'LL SEE A COCK AND SOME BUSH AND A BIT OF TIT.'

'*JAMES BLUNT: THE MUSICAL* IS A TRIUMPH.'

'IF YOU'RE A POOF, YOU'LL LOVE THIS.'

'*WE WILL ROCK YOU*, STARRING BARRY GEORGE.'

'*EQUUS* – YOUR CHANCE TO SEE HARRY POTTER'S COCK.'

'CRASH BANG WALLOP! WHAT A FUCKING NIGHTMARE,
I'VE DROPPED MY LAPTOP.'

'YOU'LL BELIEVE A MAN CAN WALK OUT AFTER FIVE MINUTES
AND ASK FOR HIS MONEY BACK.'

'IT MOVED ME TO TEARS . . . IT WAS SO BORING.'

'*THE VAGINA MONOLOGUES* IS A WORLDWIDE PHENOMENON,
HAVING STARRED THE LIKES OF KATE WINSLET,
JERRY HALL, WHOOPI GOLDBERG AND SHARON STONE.
NOW IT COMES TO YOUR TOWN WITH, ERR . . . JENNY ECLAIR
AND MARLENE FROM *ONLY FOOLS AND HORSES*.'

'NEW *CHITTY CHITTY BANG BANG* – YOU'LL BELIEVE
A CAR CAN FLY AND THAT PEOPLE CAN'T ACT.'

'PETER SUTCLIFFE IS A REVELATION.'

'FROM THE MAKERS OF *MISS SAIGON* COMES:
MISS DARFUR.'

'ABU HAMZA IS THE BEST FIDDLER SINCE TOPOL.'

'*THE PAULA RADCLIFFE STORY* WILL RUN AND RUN.'

'I MASTURBATED ALL THE WAY THROUGH.'

'I COULDN'T STOP CRYING WHEN I REALISED
HOW MUCH I PAID FOR THIS TICKET.'

'AS THE TIGER DEVOURED ROY, YOU COULD HEAR THE AUDIENCE
STUNNED BY THE DUO'S STAGECRAFT . . .'

'RONNIE CORBETT IS A BOLD CHOICE TO PLAY OTHELLO.'

'WHAT *MAMMA MIA* DID FOR ABBA,
THIS WILL DO FOR ANAL SEX.'

BOOKS HEADED STRAIGHT FOR THE BARGAIN BIN

How to Grow Old with Dignity – Peter Stringfellow

The Curious Incident of Dogging at Night-time

The A to B of London

The Pop-Up Nude Camilla

Ventriloquism for Dummies

My Struggle – Paris Hilton

Down and Out in Paris Hilton

100 Great Guinea Pig Recipes

Lady Thatcher's Lover

The Rough Guide to Helmand

Dennis Potter and the Goblet Of Fire

Pimp My Bookcase

George Best: The Idiotic Drunken Twat

Raising Flies

How Clean Is Your Spouse?

Eats, Shoots and Leaves: US Foreign Policy

How to Make the Best of a Death Sentence

How to Get Your Luggage on a Plane

Families and How to Survive Them – Princess Diana

Stephen Hawking's Deadly Art of Unarmed Combat

Prince Edward's Guide to Starting a Small Business

Shag Yourself Thin – John Prescott

Pete Doherty's Scratch 'n' Sniff

How to Write a Postcard – a Step By Step Guide (Volume 1)

100 Great Tube Journeys

Lizards of Wales

John Betjeman's Sex Life in Pictures

Drainspotting

Roy Keane's Little Book of Calm

I Did it My Way – Tord Grip

UNLIKELY COMPLAINTS TO THE BBC

Dear BBC, what happened to that nice Lesley Grantham? Bring him back. And why no Michael Barrymore? More, please.

Dear BBC, I must complain most strongly about your programme *Points of View* – it gives a platform to gibbering lunatics from the Home Counties. Less, please.

Dear BBC, I once saw a very amusing piece of footage showing the Queen storming away from the throne. Why hasn't it been repeated, over and over again?! Yours, Mr C. Windsor.

Dear BBC, it has also been fifty-five years since you last showed a Coronation – isn't it about time we had another one?! Yours, Mr C. Windsor.

'Stop me or I'll kill again.' Sorry, shouldn't have read that one out.

Dear BBC, given the success of retro shows such as *Strictly Come Dancing*, wouldn't it be a good idea to bring back the good old *Black and White Minstrel Show*?

Dear BBC, I find it most frustrating that just as it gets to a crucial point in *Eastenders*, some drums start playing and the episode's over. It's quite maddening as I then have to watch the next one.

Dear BBC, what was that music you played over the collapse of the Twin Towers? My friend says it was Showaddywaddy – but I lean towards the Rubettes.

Dear BBC, are you interested in penis enlargement?

Dear BBC, I laughed and laughed and laughed until Huw Edwards stopped reading the news.

Dear BBC, can we please have more programmes with minor celebrities doing everyday things? Yours, Don Estelle from *It Ain't Half Hot Mum*.

Dear BBC, has Eamonn Holmes lost weight? It doesn't look like it to me.

Dear BBC, isn't it time for 4 Poofs and a Piano to get their own show? Yours, The Fat One.

Dear *Points of View*, I have very much enjoyed the latest series of *Anal Adventures*. In fact, I'm watching it now with my trousers round my ankles – here's hoping no one sees me standing outside Dixons.

Dear BBC, shame on you. Last night, you showed a baby seal being clubbed to death, but stopped the film just before the interesting bit. Can you show it, please?

REJECTED EXAM QUESTIONS

1. Please give examples.

2. Describe the reproductive system of the frog without getting an erection.

3. Jane Austen was an anteater. She was. How do you know? Were you there? No. So there. Discuss.

4. Out a gay member of staff at your school using hearsay, maliciousness and homophobia.

5. It is red and itches a bit, but has stopped throbbing since Thursday. What the fuck is wrong with me? For extra marks: should I see a doctor?

6. Baljit and Susan are working together to help Wang dig a hole. Express as a percentage how politically correct this question is.

7. How easy are GCSEs, man?

8. Why do fools fall in love? Give examples with references to birds singing gay.

9. If Mary had £1 million in savings in 1976 and invested half at a rate of 5 per cent and the other half at a rate of 7 per cent in 1992, but lost it all last year, calculate her total losses and why the fuck I married her.

10. What do you prefer? Jazz or jam? Please show your workings.

11. Complete this sequence: 1, 2, 3, 4, 5, 6, 7, 8 . . .

12. Compare the methods of characterization and plot development in *The Da Vinci Code* with the Highway Code.

13. Using only the English language, please write something.

14. What has been the the greater weapon in political dialogue in the last few years – bathos, rhetoric or blackmail?

15. Discuss Shakespeare's use of nocturnal imagery in *The Tempest* with reference to the stuff you wrote on your arm last night when revising.

16. Humpty Dumpty sat on the wall. Humpty Dumpty had a great . . . ?

17. Which of these options should you do if you are happy and you know it?

18. Name a business like showbusiness.

19. Complete this sequence by writing in your PIN number.

20. Give the person behind you oral sex using tongue, teeth and saliva.

21. Are you going to vote Labour when you're older? We'll give you an A*.

22. Write your name here. Please show your workings.

23. Is it me or is it stuffy in here? Discuss.

24. 4, 4, 4, 3, 1, 2, 1, 2, 1. What is the next number in this sequence of Arsenal's league position under Arsene Wenger?

25. Do you suffer from memory loss? Call this number for a free month's trial of our kit.

UNAPPETISING THINGS TO READ ON A MENU

Vegetarian option: something horrible with tofu

Tin de Hoops de Spaghetti

Poulet à la Flu

Potato stuffed inside a pig's arse

No exchanging, no sharing, no kindness of any sort

Today's Special: Whole Cow (select your own)

Whole sea bass at market price
(but it's a seriously expensive market)

Today's set menus:
1. 'Wow! That's Pricey'
2. 'You Have to Be Kidding'
3. 'Fuck me!'

*Indicates low fat   **Indicates low fat and tasteless

Japanese breakfast: some bitter things
and some stuff with the consistency of snot

Select your own fish and then butcher it, you heartless bastard

UNPOPULAR COCKTAILS

The Long Slow Uncomfortable Screw Against a Wheelie Bin

Cup-a Sick *(soup, cup, absinthe)*

Bald Russian *(tea, sushi, polonium-210, the KGB)*

The Winehouse *(gin, hair, heroin, coke, you name it and more gin)*

Sex in an Alleyway *(bucket of alcohol, holiday in Ibiza, Essex girl)*

Overpriced Health Drink *(a carrot, water, large bill)*

On the Blob *(moods, snaps, tantrums, appetite)*

Low-Budget Holiday *(uncooked meat, unwashed hands, rinse in water supply, add a dash to the toilet, can help weight loss)*

The Almond Surprise *(amyl nitrite, bucket of jizz, stomach pump)*

The Exchange-Rate Mechanism *(very dry gin, remove gin)*

Phlegm Punch *(turkey, Tamiflu, H5N1)*

The Doherty *(drugs, alcohol, junk food, shaken but won't stir)*

The Prescott *(lager, chips, brown sauce, chipolata, cocktail umbrella, don't worry if you haven't got the cocktail umbrella)*

THINGS YOU WOULDN'T HEAR
ON CHILDREN'S TV

'This is a picture sent in by nine-year-old Jane Davies. Nine? Bloody hell, I'd have said she was four. It's shit.'

'T is for twat, as in, "The producer, who is not renewing my contract, is a twat".'

'Frida is ready to hibernate and she'll be asleep for a long time, because someone not a million miles away from me drove their big flashy car over her in the BBC car park last night.'

'In this episode of *Hannah Montana* she discovers the fifteen-year-old boy she's been emailing is actually a forty-two-year-old lorry driver.'

'We're digging up the flower beds for the first time since 1987 to see . . . ooh, what's this? Shit, it's a skull, arrggh.'

'What's the matter?' said Pat. 'I've got loads of letters still to deliver.'
    'Try fucking indicating next time, you four-eyed twat.'

'And you take the fish like this and bite the head off, feel the warm blood ooze down your chin, mmm . . .'

'Every night, beneath the Arches of Waterloo Bridge, lies Andy Pandy, once one of the biggest stars on TV, now forgotten and fighting an increasingly hopeless battle with the bottle.'

'This is 'snot'.'

'That was the blue one, it's kind of smooth and mellow, this small purple one gives you more of a buzz.'

'Rupert, me Tiger Lily, me love you long time.'

'Tonight on *Science Quest*: is it safer to take it up the arse?'

'Edna the cow was crying.
　　"Why so sad?" said Sammy the sheep.
　　"Well, all my family are burning on that pyre over there."
　　"You'll be next," said Sammy. "Here's the DEFRA man – scarper".'

'That was sent in by Iqbal Qasim. It wasn't really, one of our researchers drew it, but it makes us look more inclusive.'

'So with that one, I now have one in every single orifice. Join me next week on *Fun with Sprouts* to see how I got on.'

'This year's expedition was to Basra. John and I wanted to get stuck in, so we put on our body armour and set off. Unfortunately, John immediately stepped on a landmine, but we have got what's left of Shep.'

'What have we got in the sack? Let's have a look . . . it's loads of hate mail and death threats for our Jewish presenter.'

SURPRISING THINGS TO READ ON A LABEL

Ironing instructions:
GET WIFE TO DO IRONING

In the collar of a pair of Oxfam pyjamas:
UNWASHED SINCE WORN ON DEATHBED

School-Dinner Swizzlers:
INGREDIENTS: STUFF, 99%; TURKEY, 1%

Dog food:
INGREDIENTS: 'LUCKY LAD', FELL AT THE FIRST, HAYDOCK

Pot Noodle:
BEST AFTER TEN PINTS

Ikea entertainment centre:
INSTRUCTIONS NOT INCLUDED,
THAT SHOULD KEEP YOU ENTERTAINED

Duchy Original Hash cakes:
MADE TO PRINCE HARRY'S OWN RECIPE

Pig scrotum:
MAY CONTAIN NUTS

Thai ladyboy:
MAY CONTAIN NUTS

Burgers:
COOKING INSTRUCTIONS:
FLAME GRILL ON BARBEQUE UNTIL CARBON

READY MEAL FOR ONE . . . SAD LONELY BASTARD

WET SUIT – DRY CLEAN ONLY

UNAPPETISING THINGS TO READ ON A MENU

Thai Soup – chicken, pork, shrimp or baby seal

Mexican-style main course*:
burrito, enchilada or taco
(*includes amoebic dysentery)

Prawn à la Sewer

A selection of steaks ruined on our barbecue

Cooked either well done, medium, medium rare
or dripping with warm life, blood still pulsing through
its twitching, pain-wracked cadaver

Duck au Ketchup

All our chickens were force fed for two months
in a cage too small to stand up in

We're obviously overcharging so just pay what you want

Fresh peaches in lard

All our beef has been humanely shot with a bolt gun,
piled in huge stacks, lightly doused in accelerant and
set alight by fully trained men in masks

THE WORST RECORDS IN THE WORLD . . . EVER!

'Mad about the Boy' by the Catholic Bishops' Choir

Ian Huntley Sings . . .

The Complete Harry Potter, read by Professor Stephen Hawking

Ann Widdecombe's 'Je T'aime'

Princes William and Harry:
'There's No One Quite Like Grandma'

The Love Ballads of Cradle of Filth

Iain Duncan Smith's Greatest Speeches

Karaoke for the Deaf

Now That's What I Call Mime!

20 Funeral Singalong Hits

'You'll Never Wank Alone'

'You're Once, Twice, Three Times Over the Legal Limit'

'A Day in the Wife'

'Eye of the Tiger' by the Chinese Herbal Medicine Choir

'I Left My Hat in San Francisco'

'I Won't Survive'

'RSPCA'

'Caesarean Rhapsody'

'Buggered for the Very First Time'

'You've Lost that Living Feeling'

'You've Got to Hide Your Porn Away'

'You Stole My Son From My Car'

'Shite Christmas'

'Wherever I Lay My Hat
(That's Usually Where it is When I Come Back)'

'Anarchy in the AA'

'Who's that C*nt?'

'Jumping Jack Flasher'

UNLIKELY THINGS TO READ IN A FORTUNE COOKIE

YOU'RE FUCKED

GOODBYE, CRUEL WORLD! LOVE, YOUR COOKIE

HELP, I'M TRAPPED IN A FORTUNE-COOKIE FACTORY

YOU'VE EATEN THIS WITHOUT OPENING IT,
YOU GREEDY BASTARD

YOU HAVE JUST PAID OVER THE ODDS
FOR A MEDIOCRE CHINESE MEAL

IF YOU'VE COME HERE FOR A MEAL ON
VALENTINE'S NIGHT, I IMAGINE YOU MUST BE
TRAPPED IN A LOVELESS MARRIAGE AND
YEARNING TO STRAY

YOU ARE ABOUT TO READ THIS OUT IN A
PATHETIC ATTEMPT AT A CHINESE ACCENT AND MAY
PREFIX IT WITH: 'CONFUCIUS HE SAY . . .'

YOU ARE ABOUT TO GIVE THE WAITER A HUGE TIP

YOU THOUGHT THAT PORK LOOKED LIKE DOG

YES, WE HAVE NICE FOOD, BUT
A QUESTIONABLE RECORD ON HUMAN RIGHTS

AN ANVIL IS SUSPENDED ABOVE YOUR HEAD,
DON'T LOOK UP – ANY SUDDEN MOVEMENT
COULD RELEASE IT

IN ORDER TO READ THIS, YOU HAVE OBLITERATED
THE COOKIE, YOU HEARTLESS BASTARD

YOUR COOKIE WILL NOW SELF-DESTRUCT

YOU HAVE BEEN CHARGED £10 FOR THIS COOKIE

PREPARE TO DIE

WE ARE FROM THE PLANET SNACK,
THAT COOKIE WAS OUR LEADER

YOU ARE GAY

THIS COOKIE IS RADIOACTIVE

THINGS YOU WOULDN'T HEAR ON CHILDREN'S TV

'Hello, I'm Uncle Pockets, come on Vanessa, come and have a delve, see what I've got, keep going, deeper, that's it, keep feeling around there, go on . . .'

'This story was sent in by Jemima White, aged seven, it's very good, so good in fact that we think your mum wrote it, so you're not having the prize. Let that be a lesson to Mrs Pushy Fucking White.'

'This week's episode of *High School Musical* has had to be cancelled as one of the pupils has gone on a rampage with a gun.'

'And on today's episode of *Clifford the Big Red Dog*, Clifford does an enormous shit in the garden.'

'Next up is *Balamory*. If you don't want to be singing the theme tune all day long, turn over now.'

'So you smear them with honey like so, and . . . let's give it a go . . . Shep, come here boy.'

'In this week's episode of *Camberwick Green*, Pugh, Pugh, Barney McGrew, Cuthbert, Dibble and Grub come under a hail of bottles as they attend a car fire on a council estate.'

'In this week's edition of *Bob the Builder*, Bob is replaced by Bogodan the builder from Poland.'

'You'll need a pair of scissors for this – so grab a pair of scissors while your mum's not looking.'

'I'm afraid the *Blue Peter* golden retriever has died – it was flattened by a ten-ton truck while shagging a spaniel on the hard shoulder.'

'Another way to make pocket money is to film your parents having sex and then post it on the Internet.'

'Oh, no, Bob the Builder – here's Vern the VAT Man.'

'Hi kids, retired and unemployed people!'

'You'll need grown-ups to help you cut this picture out – as you won't be allowed to buy the porn mag yourself.'

'Hi kids, no one presents kids' telly because they want to.'

'Next on *Blue Peter* – what to do with half a ton of elephant shit.'

'Sadly, Fireman Sam's breathing equipment was faulty . . .'

'Here comes Gordon, the big homosexual engine . . . with a tender behind.'

'This is my last *Play School* because my bastard ex-boyfriend has posted a video of me snorting coke and giving him a blow job on the Internet. Bye.'

'"It's not true about them having nine lives, then," said Pat, having accidentally reversed over Jess . . .'

'So, Scooby, the janitor wasn't pretending to be a mummy, he just had terrible burns from a recent accident.'

BAD THINGS TO SAY ON A FIRST DATE

'Let's share the peas. One for you, one for me, one for you, one for me . . .'

'Before I offer to pay the bill, can I just check that we are going to have sex later?'

'How many children do you want?'

'You don't drink? Oh, fucking hell!!'

'My favourite colour – spurting-blood red I think.'

'Let's have lunch here, then go on to the *Doctor Who* convention.'

'We can go back to my place, my wife's a heavy sleeper.'

'To mark our first date I'd like to return the underwear I stole off your washing line.'

'The tie? Why, it's made from the skin of my former victims.'

'Sorry about that, I've followed through. I hope you're upwind.'

'Yes, it is a gun in my pocket.'

'Just wait while I switch my camera on.'

'I hope you like dogs – I'm serving one with rice and salad.'

'I'd like to sit down, but as you'll find out, I've got a prolapsed anus.'

'I like big women – why are you crying?'

'You're strong, aren't you? The drugs should have started to work by now.'

'My favourite film director? I don't know – who made *Shaven Vixens VI*?'

'Shall we go Dutch? You can come back to my place and sit naked in the window.'

'I'll order a bottle of the house red, and would you like anything to drink?'

'Wow! Let me just look at you in that low-cut top. HONK HONK.'

'Would you like to come back to my place for a quick night cock, sorry, cap?'

'I'm not like other men – I'm a violent rapist.'

'I think it's sweet that you're a vegetarian. I'll have the sheep's brains and tripe, please.'

'I didn't have any rice so I'm not paying for that.'

'I'd suggest dinner, but I'm not allowed cutlery.'

SURPRISING THINGS TO READ ON A LABEL

Chicken:
INGREDIENTS: 70% SALMONELLA, 30% WATER

MADE IN GREAT BRITAIN

HAND-STITCHED BY ABU HAMZA

PARENTAL GUIDANCE:
YOU WILL BE MORE OFFENDED THAN YOUR CHILDREN

HIGHLY FLAMMABLE – OR DO I MEAN INFLAMMABLE?
OH GOD, I NEVER KNOW THE DIFFERENCE

BEST BEFORE YESTERDAY

Turkey cooking time:
TWO HOURS LONGER THAN YOU EXPECT

SERVES TWO – IF YOU'RE NOT VERY HUNGRY

SIZE 14 (SIZE 4 AFTER A WASH)

CAUTION: MAY CONTAIN NUTS, MILK OR WHEAT,
YOU SAD ALLERGIC BASTARDS

CONTAINS WHEAT, GLUTEN, SOYA, BARLEY
AND FREE CHOKING HAZARD

GOURMET CRISPS – JUST HOW MUCH
WILL YOU PAY FOR ONE POTATO?

ILL-ADVISED CHATROOM NAMES

PAEDO IN DISGUISE

UNDERCOVER POLICEMAN

SCROTUMFACE

MAHMOUD AHMADINEJAD

VALERIE SINGLETON

SMALLDICK

I'M REALLY A MINGER

TERRORIST MASTERMIND

RACIST

RT HON. GORDON BROWN MP

IGNORE ME

HAROLD SHIPMAN'S GHOST

LEMBIT OPIK

MUSHROOM ARSE

HIGH ON METHS

ON THE VERGE OF SUICIDE

DRUG DEALER

NOT REALLY 12, I'M 54

ASSASSINATE OBAMA

W**KF**KS**TC**T

UNLIKELY AGONY AUNT LETTERS

Auntie, I'm in agony, love, your nephew.

Dear Agony Aunt, I keep getting dangerous advice from hugely unqualified people – what do you suggest I do?

Dear Agony Aunt, please help me, I can't stop making up bullshit problems and sending them to newspaper agony aunts.

Dear Agony Aunt, I think my wife may no longer love me. I enclose a series of pictures of her in her underwear and me in briefs discussing our problems, which you might want to turn into a photo story.

Dear Agony Aunt, I can't stop masturbating over agony aunt columns.

Dear Agony Aunt, I have a very tiny penis, which is not good – but I am a woman, which is worse.

Dear Agony Aunt, I am worried about losing some sensitive government data that it is my job to safeguard, so I have sent it to you to look after.

Dear Agony Aunt, is it true you can't get pregnant if your boyfriend gives you an STD?

Dear Agony Aunt, this is a genuine letter.

Dear Agony Aunt, I'm having an affair with the husband of your paper's agony aunt.

Dear Agony Aunt, I have a problem with premature ejaculation . . . whoops, sorry, have to go now.

Dear Agony Aunt, I suffer from Tourette's, you fucking c*nt.

Dead Agony Ant, my spell chocker brock, whit shull I do.

Dear Agony Aunt, I'm a serial killer obsessed with stalking and then killing agony aunts. I am typing this on your home computer.

Dear Agony Aunt, it's tough being the world's most intelligent dog.

Dear Agony Aunt, I am painfully shy – will it do me any good to publicize my problem in a national newspaper?

Dear Agony Aunt, I am not quite pretty enough to appear on page three – can you please use me in one of your photo stories?

Dear Agony Aunt, I'm a gay man, but I'm neither witty nor stylish – am I secretly straight?

LINES CUT FROM A SUPERHERO FILM

'Sorry, Lois, I did warn you I was faster than a speeding bullet.'

'You know Batman, sometimes you remind me of that poncey rich twat Bruce Wayne.'

'Unfortunately, Superman was using his X-ray vision and has flown directly into that wall.'

'Holy Inappropriate, Batman, you're hurting me!'

'Sorry, I've got web all over the sheets, I'll sleep in that bit.'

'Look, Commissioner Gordon, I don't want to give you advice, but could we not keep the Joker, the Riddler and the Penguin in prison for more than a week?'

'How unlucky – he escaped to Earth from his doomed planet but his capsule landed on Krakatoa at the precise moment it erupted.'

'Holy Fucking Shit, Batman.'

'I put out the fire Lois, by ejaculating over it from my super gonads.'

'Catwoman, will you use the litter tray, for fuck's sake.'

'It's a shame that there's one bit of your body that doesn't extend, Elastic Man.'

'I have further evidence that Batman hit my client, M'Lud. Exhibit three: a large sign saying, 'Whack'.'

'I've used my laser vision to microwave that sandwich.'

'You're not exactly striking fear into the hearts of the city's criminals, Mediocreman.'

'How exactly *do* you fly, Captain Flatulence?'

'Look! There! In the sky! Is it a bird? Is it a plane? No, it's Birdplane Man!'

'Dr Banner, I'm afraid you can't come to my Anger Management seminar any more.'

'We're the X Men and we're looking for our X wives.'

'I used to be faster than a speeding bullet, but I did my anterior cruciate ligament.'

'According to my X-ray vision, you require a filling in your right upper molar.'

'A happy finish, please, Alfred.'

'Hollywood seems to be down to the less well-known Marvel characters now, Scraping the Barrel Man . . .'

'We've had to let the Joker go under the Human Rights Act.'

'You're late, Virgintrainman.'

'Robin, stop being a bat c*nt.'

UNLIKELY THINGS TO FIND WRITTEN ON A SHAMPOO BOTTLE

WARNING: DO NOT USE ON HAIR.

WHY ARE YOU READING THIS SHAMPOO BOTTLE?

TESTED ON ANIMALS. THEIR EYES FELL OUT
BUT THEIR HAIR LOOKED LOVELY.

CONTAINS EXTRACT OF AVOCADO,
THOUGH TO BE HONEST WE'VE NO IDEA IF THAT'S
A GOOD THING OR NOT.

MAY CAUSE ALOPECIA.

MAY CONTAIN TRACES OF ASBESTOS.

FOR REALLY DISGUSTING, GREASY HAIR.

40% PROOF.

SEE DOCTOR IN CASE OF CONTACT WITH SKIN.

CAUTION: DO NOT GET WET.

YOUR HAIR IS SHIT.

INSTRUCTIONS FOR USE:
IT'S SHAMPOO, FOR CHRIST'S SAKE!
WORK IT OUT FOR YOURSELF.

IDEAL FOR ITCHY SCALPS.
GUARANTEED TO GIVE YOU ONE.

CONTAINS ESSENTIAL OILS
FOR SHINY HAIR AND A WET NOSE.

WITH EXTRACT OF VANILLA,
FOR PEOPLE WHO LIKE THEIR HAIR
TO SMELL LIKE CUSTARD.

CONTENTS: SHAMPOO.

FOR MATURE LADIES,
TO HELP COLOUR THOSE GREY HAIRS.
ALSO AVAILABLE IN MINGE-SIZED BOTTLES.

CONTAINS EXTRACT OF JOJOBA,
AND EXTRACT OF HOBO.

THIS SHAMPOO CAN HELP YOU
FLICK YOUR HAIR AROUND IN SLOW-MOTION
AS OFTEN AS YOU WANT.

WILL MAKE YOUR HAIR LOOK LOVELY
– WE'RE TELLING YOU THIS IN CASE YOU
GET ANY IN YOUR EYES AND GO BLIND.

REJECTED EXAM QUESTIONS

1. Was your reaction to the previous question
   a) 'Yeesss!', b) 'Hmmm', or c) 'Shiiittt!'?

2. Using the mirror provided, copy the answer off that lad next to you.

3. Use the pen and paper provided to do some maths and stuff.

4. If Chris robs Peter to pay Paul, why did he get involved in this process in the first place?

5. Show us your tits for an automatic A*.

6. You're shit, and you know you are. Discuss.

7. Peter is older than John and John is older than Mary, but they are all far too young to be doing what I'm paying them for. How long am I going to get?

8. Think of a number, double it, take two, add three, divide by two, multiply by five, add three, take away six. Have you got the number you first thought of? You haven't? Bollocks, it normally works.

9. How many words do you have to change from an answer downloaded off the Internet to not be accused of cheating?

10. Parlez-vous français? Answer: a) oui, b) 31, c) an elephant.

11. Why is it when your exam results come out the papers only print pictures of pretty girls?

12. John has a knife, Peter has a gun but no knife, Andy has a knife, a gun and an axe. Which gangs are they in?

13. Rewrite *War and Peace* using words of one syllable but making it better than Tolstoy's original.

14. Shakespeare is shit and that innit. Discuss.

15. If John who is 5 ft 11 in. tall bumps into Paul who is 5 ft 7 in. in the pub, calculate the angle Paul would need to raise a 7 in. pint glass to stab John in the face.

16. In no more than 1,000 words write out 'Pointless' 1,000 times.

17. If my dad is bigger than your dad, what the fuck are you going to do about it?

18. If Michael spent £800,000 on a house 18 months ago and that house has decreased 37 per cent in value, calculate how long Michael will be able to resist alcoholism and suicide.

19. Mark has lost a leg but grown an arm. Peter has lost a head and grown two legs. Which one will be the subject of a Channel 4 documentary first?

20. Chemistry – what percentage of Jordan is silicon?

21. If your midfielder is worth £20 million, how much do you inflate the price when Man City enquire about him?

22. Insert the following up your anus and chart the results on a bar graph.

23. What is the 654th word of the sixth *Harry Potter* book?

24. Jeremy Kyle – why?

25. Haven't you finished yet, you moron?

BAD THINGS TO SAY ON A FIRST DATE

'You remind me of my eighth wife.'

'No alcohol for me – I'm trying to get pregnant.'

'I'm stuffed – I can't eat another thing. Not if you're expecting anal.'

'No one knows where you are, do they?'

'No food for me, thanks, I'll just have wine.'

'I'll have a dump before eating. I don't need to move, I'm wearing a nappy.'

'Flowers for a lovely lady – I took a shortcut via the graveyard.'

'I'm a bit of a regular here – I can thoroughly recommend the Happy Meal.'

'If you didn't want me looking down your top you shouldn't have worn one so low-cut. Anyway, I'd better get back to my date now.'

'I've been told it's cleared up so I can't wait to try it out.'

'I thought it best if we met in a disused warehouse.'

'Would you like to come back to my place and see my life-size matchstick model of Barry George?'

'I never wear underwear – it aggravates my genital rash.'

'Please don't ask me if that dress makes you look fat.'

'You are so sexy, will you excuse me while I go to the bathroom and masturbate?'

BAD NAMES FOR RESTAURANTS

BEEF CURTAINS

SAM & ELLA'S

NOROVIRUS

LEFTOVERS

OFFAL WORLD

SPROUT-U-LIKE

YO DOGGY!

PISS HUT

IT'LL DO

BATTERY-FARMED FRIED CHICKEN

MAD COWS

RETCHERS

CRIPPEN'S CHOP HOUSE

LITVINENKO'S

CANNIBAL HUT

UNSUCCESSFUL JOB APPLICATIONS

I am a team player – in fact, I'm probably the single best team player in the country.

You must hire me, before I kill again!

I am conscientious, hardworking, tenacious, etc., etc.

I understand you're an Equal Opportunities employer, so I bet you've got some cracking birds in the office.

I have a lot of experience of charity work – I'm one of those annoying people on the street with sweatshirts and clipboards.

Dear Conservative Selection Committee, I didn't go to Eton – does it matter?

I am highly computer literate, with an excellent working knowledge of ZX Spectrum, Casio FX21, and Amstrad skills.

Having been on ten previous missions, I bring a wealth of experience to the art of suicide bombing.

In my free time, I enjoy being a scout leader, a choirmaster and going on the Internet.

My greatest achievement? Level 37, Super Mario Galaxy Racer.

I have a Duke of Edinburgh award – I've insulted a lot of Chinese people.

Despite my lack of medical qualifications, I feel that gynaecology is a calling.

Full-time catering experience, 1987–2005 Wormwood Scrubs kitchen trustee, E Wing.

Please consult my CV – or Cunnilingus Vitae.

I'm a black lesbian in a wheelchair – how many more boxes do you want to tick?

I love to work closely with animals – you may have seen some of my work on the Internet.

I believe I should be given this job and all the major responsibilities it entails, because, you never know, it could be a laugh.

I'd like to join the army because there's nothing I like more than the sight of other men in uniform.

Dear Mrs Johnson, I am 18, Swedish and beautiful and I'd love to work as an au pair for you and Boris.

Hobbies: Wining and dining, dancing, narcotics, trawling motorway service stations, taxidermy.

I worked very hard to get to the top of my father's company.

. . . and here's a link to photos of me throwing up on Facebook.

I have a full array of computer skills. Look at the way I've Photoshopped your face into this highly unusual threesome.

UNLIKELY NATIONAL HOLIDAYS

VICTORY IN IRAQ DAY

NATIONAL HAEMORRHOID WEEK

PMT DAY OF ANGER

DIANA & DODI DAY

WANK WEEK

MANIC MONDAY

RAINY DAY

SUNDAY BLOODY SUNDAY

NEW SERIES OF GRAHAM NORTON AWARENESS
WEEK

ROLF HARRIS ARRIVAL IN BRITAIN DAY

SADDAM: 'WE GOT HIM' DAY

FESTIVAL OF SHITS

BLOW JOB THURSDAY

RAY STUBBS'S FIRST *FOOTBALL FOCUS* DAY

STOP BLOODY MOANING DAY

WHAT A GAY DAY

TITS OUT TUESDAY

HALF PRICE DAY AT DFS

DARREN DAY

BAD *QUESTION TIME* QUESTIONS

'Can I just ask David Cameron what measures he will take as Prime Minister to wipe that smug grin off his face?'

'The usual panel this week – a Labour MP, a Tory MP, a Lib Dem you've never heard of, a hard-faced businesswoman and David Baddiel.'

'I'd like to ask Alistair Darling a question, but only so I can say 'Darling' in the question and get a cheap laugh.'

'Next clichéd whinge, please.'

'I'd like to ask Hazel Blears . . . where are you? STAND UP.'

'I'd like to ask Geoff Hoon if he knows where the bogs are, please?'

'Are you related to Richard Dimbleby?'

'Can I have a round of applause, please?'

'Does anyone on the panel have a cock as big as this?'

'Samantha Cameron, you would, wouldn't you?'

'Are you trying to seduce me, Mr Dimbleby?'

'If we are a cross-section of society, does that really mean that the country is full of ugly, ill-informed people?'

'Has everyone on the panel got their brown wings?'

'Does this blouse go with these trousers?'

REJECTED EXAM QUESTIONS

1. Chemistry paper 2, question 1: using fertilizers and cleaning products, construct a bomb that can wipe out class 4B.

2. List your most sordid desires.

3. Tell me where the money is, all of it.

4. 'Bismarck was good for his country.' Ignore.

5. From memory, draw a picture of the Queen's bum.

6. If Pete has three ounces and Steve has seven, who will earn most at a nightclub?

7. 'David Miliband is a socialist icon.' Dismiss.

8. It takes two men ten minutes to check in for their flight – how long will it take Ahmed and Imran?

9. I wandered lonely as a what?

10. Do you suffer from erectile dysfunction?

11. If a budget flight leaves Stansted airport for its advertised destination of Stockholm but is actually due to land 100 miles away in neighbouring Denmark, how much money will you be refunded for the fact that the flight ends up being cancelled anyway?

12. Rearrange this sequence into the correct order: Sensibility and Sense.

13. What is courage? Putting 'this is' is not acceptable.

14. If you fail to get a grade A on this paper, what minuscule percentage of the population do you represent?

15. 'The use of computers makes students lazy.' Discuss, cutting and pasting your answer here.

16. What sells more copies of the *Daily Express*: house prices, or Diana's death?

17. Describe how Newton's laws of motion affect the aerial flight of a sphere, if the seam down the middle has been picked at by a cheating foreign bowler.

18. English Literature GCSE, Question 1: Discuss the use of imagery and metaphor in *My Story So Far* by Wayne Rooney.

19. Thunderbirds are what?

BAD THINGS TO SAY AT A ROYAL STATE BANQUET

'What the fuck is this?'

'You're the French ambassador? Yeah, right.'

'What do you mean, 'Stop slurping?''

'Pull my finger.'

'I'll just have a lager top please, chief.'

'Stand up if you hate the French.'

'Agggh, a dog, kill it, kill it.'

'You're that rich bastard who shot my osprey.'

'Prince Philip, do you know Mr Al Fayed?'

'Christ, you just get bloody comfortable and you have to get up for the national anthem. Is this going to happen every time one of them comes back from a crap?'

'Which twat got the last spud?'

'I mean, when it comes down to it, what does Andrew actually do?'

'Three German officers crossed the Rhine, parlez-vous . . .'

'You know the mentally retarded one in the forties? What happened to her?'

'Yeah? Well I'm Emperor of the Universe.'

'I'm not sitting next to him.'

(Ting ting ting). 'Can I just say on behalf of all of us, a great big thank you to Her Majesty for a cracking spread.'

LINES YOU WOULDN'T WANT TO HEAR
IN A COSTUME DRAMA

'Why, Mr Darcy, I declare from your breeches you have a cock the size of a baby's arm holding a peach.'

'Candleford's a bit of a shithole, isn't it? I'm moving to Lark Rise.'

'Well, it may be Bleak, but it's not got planning permission.'

'Yes, I shall marry you! I shall be proud to carry the name of Mrs Pockle-Thickle-Facklethwaite.'

'Miss Dashwood, I've brought round a Chinese.'

'Robin Steven Hood, I am arresting you on a charge of robbing the rich to give to the poor. You have the right to remain silent.'

'Forget about who dances with whom at some stupid sodding ball, woman, we're at war with France!'

'The main Lark Rise to Candleford road is closed this morning after a stagecoach jack-knifed and shed its load of bonnet-wearing spinsters.'

'Sorry, Mr Rochester, I'm not putting out until your wife snuffs it.'

'Why, Mr Darcy, you're piss-wet through.'

'OK, Oliver, can you show us where Mr Bumble touched you?"'

BAD *QUESTION TIME* QUESTIONS

'Can I just illustrate that I haven't understood anything anyone has said on this topic?'

'I'd like to ask Ruth Kelly if she's a boy or a girl.'

'Does anyone want to shag me?'

'Can I paraphrase what the man here just said but get it a bit wrong?'

'I'd like to ask the panel if they've got a trite but populist answer to this question that will guarantee a round of applause?'

'I'd like to ask, are Lib Dems becoming forgettable? That question to, er, whatsisname at the end, next to the Tory.'

'Do the panel think David Dimbleby should be replaced?'

'I'd like to ask the panel: what do they think about when they're knocking one out?'

'If the panel were a fish what fish would they be, and why? That question to number one.'

'I'd like to ask the Prime Minister what he would do if he wasn't such a useless twat.'

'Another question – yes, you Sir, the absurdly gay man at the back.'

'What are your favourite colours?'

'I'd like to ask the panel – are they aware the Carling Cup highlights are on the other side?'

'Welcome to the programme that looks like democracy but is really cheap entertainment for the angry.'

'Welcome to a *Question Time* special, where all the guests are naked.'

'Which member of the audience would like to have their intelligence insulted next?'

'I'd like to ask the minister what it's like to be shat on by a rent boy.'

'With respect, Harriet Harman, you're evading the question. Just what colour panties are you wearing?'

'I disagree with David Miliband's answer, would he like to come outside and discuss it further in the car park?'

'I've just popped in from the *Weakest Link* studio next door, can any of the panel tell me what 'B' is a country in South America? Brazil or Argentina?'

'Just time for one last question. Yes, you sir.'
    'I would like to ask the panel if they feel that last questions are sometimes a bit of an anti-climax?'

UNLIKELY PROPERTY MAGAZINE ADS

Beautiful North London villa – great potential if you can get rid of any of the 49 Kosovan gangsters currently squatting there.

FOR SALE: straw house and stick house. Both in need of renovation. Apply brick house. No wolves.

Deceptively large bungalow with extensive sewing and lepidoptery facilities, large ground-floor pit, would suit *Silence of the Lambs* fan.

Three foot square, would suit short and thin person.

Bijou cottage with views of town abbatoir.

Paedophile's dream: luxury apartment with unspoilt view of playground of local primary school and situated within a three-minute walk of nearest sweet shop.

At the centre of a busy community – of rock-wielding hoodies.

ACT NOW. Before they find out I didn't get planning permission.

Loud, pink, flamboyant apartment, ideal for poofs.

'Get back to nature' with wonderful opportunity to acquire unique 4,000 square foot apartment with no walls or roof.

They say it's uninhabitable, come and prove them wrong.

A stunning, unspoilt, remote location ideal for someone on the run from the police or who will never need post, shopping or assistance from the emergency services.

The wonderfully appointed lounge has beautiful red spattered wall decoration and floors and a charming chalk outline human figure in the middle of the floor.

Wake up under the stars with this spacious riverside two-zip luxury one-tog sleeping bag, within easy reach of Waterloo Bridge, oil-fired central heating provided via rusty can with holes in.

Deluxe ground-floor flat, own patio, garden and Grade II listed plague pit.

House bought as seen with fixtures, fittings and murder trial evidence.

Beautiful rural property with own swimming pool (for a month every year when the river bursts).

Priced for quick sale as owner needs to flee country.

LOT FOR SALE: Salisbury Plain. Located in the middle of the sought-after Firing Range area.

UNLIKELY T-SHIRT SLOGANS

I'M AN ANNOYING TEENAGER
WHO THINKS T-SHIRT SLOGANS ARE FUNNY

I ♥ TRANSPLANT

MY BOYFRIEND WENT TO IBIZA
AND ALL HE BROUGHT ME BACK
WAS THIS LOUSY SYPHILIS

CERTIFIED SEX INSTRUCTOR
(THOUGH OBVIOUSLY I'M STILL A VIRGIN)

IF YOU CAN READ THIS, YOU PROBABLY
WEREN'T STATE EDUCATED

THIS ISN'T A T-SHIRT, JUST A REALLY BRUTAL WEDGIE

ALL POLICEMEN ARE RACISTS

MAX MOSLEY SMACKED MY ARSE

PUNCH ME IF YOU THINK YOU'RE HARD ENOUGH

GIULIANI FOR PRESIDENT!

HERE, LOOK AT MY TITS

THIS ISN'T RED, I'VE JUST BEEN STABBED BY A HOODIE

UNLIKELY LINES FROM A SCI-FI FILM

'Quick, his battery is running out!'

'On my planet, this is considered a big dick.'

'I think I've discovered the monster's weakness – it's the zip at the back.'

'This is the planet Onan, the locals died out . . . unsurprisingly.'

'Look we can transport matter across the galaxy with this new Fax Machine.'

'Your alien language doesn't use the letters K or Z.'

'Mr Spock, you have the bridge. I'm just going for a dump.'

'I am from the planet Minge.'

'I feel a great disturbance in the force, Luke – it's almost as if someone's planning on making three dreadful prequels.'

'Luke, I am your father, cousin, uncle and brother.'

'I don't wish to criticize, Lord Vader – but I don't think a cape is terribly practical for space travel.'

'We're flying back on EasyUFO, so we aren't landing on Mars, we're actually landing on Saturn and going the rest of the way by coach.'

LINES YOU WOULDN'T WANT TO HEAR IN A COSTUME DRAMA

'The Duchess is a lady of great moral rectitude, though I understand she goes like Stevenson's Rocket.'

'Take me, take me – in about thirty minutes, when I've got all these layers of clothing off . . .'

'Your kind offer is both timely and indeed generous and should you, in all earnest, possess the wherewithal to vouchsafe its imminent presentation, I hazard to suggest it would be by no means unwelcome . . . and could you put milk and two sugars in it?'

'You haven't paid for your papers, Mr Pickwick.'

'Yes, Darcy was haughty at the Meryton ball, but so what? He's loaded and hung like a donkey.'

'Tom Jones is late, but it's not unusual.'

'This was the Old Curiosity Shop, but it's been bought by Subway.'

'Pls sir. I wd luv some more. Txt me back lol.'

'But, Miss Pendleton, this is a scene the Channel 4 commissioner insisted must be added – now get those bloomers off and join me in the lake.'

'Young Master Pip, you needn't visit upon me tonight, I'm going to stay in with my rampant rabbit.'

'That elderly spinster from the village – wasn't she M from the James Bond films?'

'Why, Mr Knightley, you've got me smelling like a fishmonger's slab.'

'Lord Fauntwell has gone outside to take the air – and try to get a signal on his mobile.'

'You have arrived here on your trusty steed, but half an hour late. So that's a guinea off my pizza.'

'I've journeyed two and a half days to get here from York. There was a contraflow on the M1.'

'You say the Brothers Karamazov have all gone to England to buy football clubs?'

'Do you like my new carriage? You'll be seeing a lot of it because we spent half the budget on it.'

'My lords and ladies, Colonel and Mrs Celebrity Walk-on. The Duke of American Co-Star for Overseas Sales. The Reverend Comedy Star Who Can't Really Act . . . and Dame Judi Dench. Again.'

'The Casterbridge Mayoral race has been thrown wide open now Boris has joined and the current Mayor is being done for funding issues.'

'We've come to take the telly and the sofa, Mrs Bennett.'

'It's true what they say about you Cranford girls.'

'Oh, Mr Micawber, when you said something would come up I didn't realize you meant that!'

'Yo, Mr Rochester, you is one slim'assed motherfucker.'

'Oh, Heathcliff, do me up the wrong'un.

TERRIBLE NAMES FOR CARS

The 4x4 Haemorrhage

The Peugeot Perineum

The Vauxhall Hawking

The Citroën Closet Homosexual

The Hyundai Affordable

The Peugeot Garlic

The Honda Scrotum

The Ford Badger

The Hatchback Deathtrap

The Robin Repugnant

The Nissan Tank Top

The Toyota Su-Doku

The Fiat Embarrassino

The Mitsubishi Dogger

The Volkswagen Risible

The Nissan Cumbersome

The Ford Schmord

The Reliant Rubber

The Renault Smoker

The Mitsubishi Smegma

The Volvo Sven

The Renault Asylum

The Volkswagen Führer

The Fiat Pederast

The Citroën Fiasco

The Lamborghini Mussolini

The BMW Smug

The Penis Substitute

The Honda Mediocre

The Renault Shipman

The Vauxhall Vulva

UNLIKELY PROPERTY MAGAZINE ADS

Come and view it, you c*nt.

Large Hackney townhouse would make ideal crack den.

Converted bungalow on airport flight path, may need renovation and possible extinguishing of still-smouldering jumbo jet.

Delightful Belfast terrace, comes with beautiful mural, metal shutters and is just a stone's throw from the lively local Catholic community.

Fully furnished flat, quick sale due to owner's leprosy.

Home in grounds of Blenheim Palace, plans for sky-scraper roller disco and stock car racetrack awaiting permission.

Frankly miserable hovel would benefit from not viewing. Don't waste your time.

Gorgeous detached property with breathtaking view of the M6 flyover.

Immaculate mansion ruined by current owner's appalling taste. Worth viewing just for a laugh.

Large leather property for sale. Wall-to-wall fitted insoles. Room for many children. Old woman owner moving to larger footwear.

Grade I listed, completely unmodernized home dating back to 55 BC, original Roman features and in need of some excavation.

House for sale bears no resemblance to picture, otherwise you wouldn't even be reading this, believe me.

TO LET: room in 1970s house share. Repeated viewing. Apply R. Rigsby.

FOR SALE: American 1960s-style, family-run motel. Shower room in need of attention.

Unusual property for sale in Far East – large industrial complex in base of subterranean volcano. Would suit evil mastermind, or young couple.

Home to one of the country's famous names – feel free to come and have a nose round whether you want to buy it or not . . . we're not supposed to tell you the owner, but the home will certainly give you some Satisfaction, he hasn't Painted it Black, but he does have some Brown Sugar in the kitchen . . .

QUESTIONS OMITTED FROM THE BRITISH CITIZENSHIP TEST

1. In a transport cafeteria, does one stub out a cigarette into the yolk or the white of an egg?

2. If someone barges ahead of you in a queue, is the correct response 'ch' or 'tt'?

3. Who has contributed most to the musical landscape of Britain: Edward Elgar, Benjamin Brittain, or Howard from the Halifax?

4. Name one Channel 4 programme apart from *Big Brother*.

5. Which side of the road should you drive on when chased by the police?

6. What volume should you set your ringtone to on the train, to ensure that everyone can hear it?

7. Just what does it say on a tin of Ronseal?

8. What is the correct etiquette for vomiting in a taxi? Kerbside window, offside window or straight on the floor?

9. What does Kerry Katona do?

10. Can you believe it's not butter?

11. Which phrase do we most popularly associate with Churchill? 'We will fight them on the beaches' or 'Oh yus'?

12. What is the correct way to see off a Jehovah's Witness?

13. How did you travel to this country?

    a) By plane

    b) Walking through the channel tunnel

    or

    c) Hiding in the back of a lorry full of tomatoes?

14. Name three insults you should shout when Frank Lampard has the ball in a football match.

15. Can you read English? If not, please go to question 19.

16. Complete the following phrase: 'Pugh, Pugh, Barney McGrew . . .'

17. For Eastern European nationals only.
    Please tick which of the following best describes you:

    a) a plumber

    b) a lap dancer

    c) a credit-card cloner

    or

    d) all of the above.

18. Are you good enough to represent this country in the 2012 Olympics? If not, can you play tennis?

19. Can you still not read bloody English?

20. Estimate to the nearest decade the age of Bruce Forsyth.

UNLIKELY LINES FROM A SCI-FI FILM

'Inland revenue, Mr Jedi – it's about your return.'

'Captain, I teleported down to the planet but I seem to have lost my cock in the process.'

'This is my watch, it is called a 'digital'.'

'Apparently Chekhov has got three sisters, if you know what I mean.'

'Hello, Big Boy. So, why do they call you 'Chewy'?'

'Look, Darth, we've just come 4,000 light years. Are you sure you left the iron on?'

'I have two hearts and fourteen anuses.'

'There he is, Officer. It's that guy from the future betting on the 3.30 at Haydock again.'

'Scotty, you've underestimated the gravity again. I think I've broken my nose on the pavement.'

'Ill-thought out, and frankly dreadful prequel, this is.'

'Earthlings, your weapons are useless against us – they're British-made.'

'My mother is from Earth but my father is a Vulcan, which is why I'm circumcised.'

'Gordon's alive, but it's not looking good.'

'Gordon's had a stroke!'

'Gordon's in a permanent vegetative state.'

'Princess Leia, you say you've never been to Earth, yet you have hair like a Danish pastry.'

'I've just seen C3PO nuts and bolts deep in R2D2.'

'The dilithium crystals, Captain – they're absolutely fine.'

'We've been hit by the Klingons – everyone wobble from left to right.'

'Captain's blog: blah blah, five-year mission, yadda yadda . . .'

'I'm from the future and I've been sent back as a matter of urgency to kill Gillian McKeith.'

'On my planet, Earth, young women greet men by putting this in their mouths and sucking repeatedly . . .'

'I told you we should have got petrol on Jupiter, but oh no, Mr Knowitall had to cut it fine . . .'

'We are from the planet Gay, we are dying out but have beautiful furnishings and a showtune collection that is second to none.'

UNLIKELY COSMETICS COMMERCIALS

'Contains boswellox, which we deliberately made
sound a bit rude.'

'Why? Because I'm incredibly shallow and thick as pig shit.'

'Hi, I'm a beauty editor, and people often ask me
what is my secret to looking young. I always say,
massive amounts of plastic surgery.'

'For proven action against wrinkles, try bathing in
the blood of young virgins nightly.'

'Our face cleanser is made with all natural ingredients.
In so much as God invented acid.'

'None of our products was tested on animals.
We use Filipino children.'

(To be read out quickly) 'This advert may be
thoroughly misleading, this product does not work at all
and may burn your face off.'

'Buy our mascara or all our lab monkeys will have
been blinded for nothing.'

'The Seven Signs of Ageing are:
incontinence, grumpiness, a musty smell, saying, 'Ooh,'
whenever you sit down, lack of knowledge of popular music,
shopping in shops selling tweed and driving in the
middle lane bang on the speed limit.'

'Hi, I'm a beauty editor, and people are always asking me
what my secret is. Well, I murdered my first husband.'

'Nivea feels good on my face and even better on my balls.'

'That's me three months ago when I was just a
pre-op transsexual.'

'My hair used to be curly and tight, now my pubes
are long and luxuriant like I've just stepped out of a salon.'

'After just one application, my blackheads are
erupting like landmines.'

'People often ask how I keep my gash looking
so neat and moist . . .'

'Why not consolidate all your looks into one
easily manageable face?'

'This woman looks fantastic – but she's a model.
You're not.'

'Try our face pack, with avocado oil and citrus extract.
Or use it as a tasty dip.'

'Our lipstick looks great on rabbits – think how good
it'll look on you!'

'Fake Tan – for when you just have to look like an
Oompa Loompa.'

'Superdrug – because, although you may be worth it,
you don't have any money.'

'I'm Heather Mills and I'm here to talk to you about
having smooth legs with Ronseal Quick Drying Woodstain.'

QUESTIONS OMITTED FROM THE BRITISH CITIZENSHIP TEST

1. For fast-track applicants: which Premiership club are you most interested in buying?

2. According to the *Daily Mail*, when resident in the UK do you intend to

   a) sponge

   b) cause trouble

   c) refuse to adapt to our bloody culture,

   or

   d) all of the above?

3. You have a credit card, but you are not in debt. Why not?

4. A couple of years ago, a BBC TV trailer portrayed the Queen as a grumpy old cow. In what way was it not telling the truth?

5. Who did put the bomp in the bomp-a-bomp-a bomp, who put the ram in the ram-a-lam-a-ding-dong?

6. What exactly is the wrong sort of snow?

7. Can you speak a foreign language? (A positive answer may not help your case.)

8. It's a sunny Sunday afternoon: what degree skin burns will you have by Monday morning?

9. What is Toad-in-the-Hole, and why?

10. Where is it better to dump an old fridge: on a street corner or in a lay-by?

11. Are either or both of your hands hooks?

12. What word is missing from this sentence: 'The M5 is . . . . this Bank Holiday Monday'?

13. Which of the Queen's children hasn't been divorced?

14. Who is more important in the *Carry On* mythos: Joan Sims or Bernard Bresslaw? Discuss.

15. You're not Mohammed al Fayed, are you?

16. Would you like to donate half a million pounds to the Labour Party? If yes, answer no further questions.

17. Who was better on Basil Brush: Mr Roy or Mr Derek?

18. To the nearest five pounds, how much should you pay for a cup of tea at a service station?

19. For how many weeks of the year are you interested in tennis?

UNLIKELY PROPERTY MAGAZINE ADS

House for sale, £25 o.n.o., original swing bin and will throw in Bounty kitchen towel.

Opportunity to purchase unique detached corrugated iron residence in London's hip up-and-coming Little Darfur region.

Enviable beachfront property benefiting from recent sudden change in location from top to bottom of cliff, in need of some rebuilding.

First time on the market since last week when I bought it off a senile old woman and am now flogging it for £100,000 more.

A once in a lifetime opportunity to purchase a secluded woodland mansion unexpectedly available due to horrendous bloodbath of previous owner and family. 25-year lease, or 16 if he behaves himself in prison.

Get in first – unbelievable apartment, very quiet, particularly after Lights Out or during Sedation Hour, planning permission pending for conversion from asylum.

Imposing, beautiful ambassador-style residence – 6 bedrooms, 4 reception rooms, 6,000 square feet, beautiful garden, planning permission for toilet (in Hampstead's famous no-bathroom conservation area).

Move up in the world. This beautiful residence boasts 15 bedrooms, indoor pool, leisure complex and carriageway parking for 20 cars – OK, it's a room at the Holiday Inn Birmingham.

Bijou apartment in highly desirable area of North London, so neighbours likely to be c*nts.

FOR SALE: designer family home on private island, swimming pool/rocket launchpad. Apply J. Tracey.

Spacious white-painted, timber-framed home, on top of large pole. Charming rustic design. 1 foot by 2. Would suit dove.

Four houses for sale – Whitechapel Road – upgrading to hotel. Dogs and top hats must not apply.

TO LET: deceptively spacious accommodation, blue wooden exterior. Ideal for policeman, or Time Lord.

Large, well-appointed dog, would suit family of fleas. Short walk to park, no chain.

FOR SALE: house. Slightly bleak. Apply C. Dickens.

Large timber-framed houseboat. Very roomy, 40 cubits by 20. Pets welcome. Leasehold 40 days and 40 nights. Apply Noah.

Small but desirable home, convenient for City and West End, located just south of Zimbabwe's main airport.

BAD THINGS TO HEAR ON A HOLIDAY PROGRAMME

'Frankly, I found the reps' blow jobs were too slurpy and toothy and I won't come again.'

'On tonight's show I'll be visiting a yoga retreat to be annoyed by lot of neurotic middle-aged women and a single predatory man.'

'I've been vaccinated against typhoid, but unfortunately John wasn't as well prepared.'

'If you want the holiday that Judith and I enjoyed on this programme then you'll have to be extremely rich.'

'You won't be pestered by local children – they're all at work in the training shoe factory.'

'Don't make the mistake of smoking in the street – if you're a woman you might just find yourself on the receiving end of death by stoning . . . like this . . . arrrgghhh . . .'

'The locals are all friendly, but not as friendly as our Algerian cameraman who I saw roughly taking Ann from behind on the terrace at 3 a.m. last night.'

'There's loads to do in the hotel, which is lucky as we haven't been allowed out since the coup.'

'What part of 'chips' don't you understand, dago?'

'Cocaine is strictly forbidden in Dubai, so you'd best bring your own.'

'You can enjoy a walking holiday in the recently cleared minefields of Mozam— boom!'

'We've come to Ibiza to study their culture – but really we've come to look at girls' breasts.'

'Don't worry if your French isn't up to standard, the locals are more than happy for you to point and shout in English.'

'This beautiful hotel with swimming pool is just one of the fantastic places your licence fee is going.'

'For some people, Thailand is just about hot weather, cheap drugs, cheap drinks and easy sex, and I'm one of those people. Let's get down to it!'

'You can find accommodation for as little as £5, but it will be shit.'

'If you're travelling through Europe this summer, remember these three basic rules: the Germans have no sense of humour, the French smell and Greeks are thieves.'

'If you enjoy a bit of 'pick your own' you'll love the opium poppy fields of Afghanistan.'

'Things were going from bad to worse as I'd been abducted by rebels and forced to fight against the Revolutionary Guard.'

THINGS YOU DON'T WANT TO HEAR ON A SEX PHONE LINE

'OK, I'm putting on my jumper . . .'

'Yer big poof.'

'I'm hung like a fieldmouse.'

'Ooh, yes, that feels good . . . sorry, I'm at the chiropractors.'

'I'm eating a bacon and egg sandwich and the brown sauce is going all over me flip-flops.'

'I'm standing at Clapham Junction and I can see the B4765 pulling in to Platform 12.'

'Hello, this sex call has been outsourced to Bangalore. Can I be helping you to come, Sir?'

'118118, would you like to be put straight through if you know what I mean, Madam?'

'This is John Prescott, and since I retired I've been contemplating the exploration of sexual fantasticat . . . oh, bollocks, pass us me mini kievs . . .'

'I'm wearing a negligee and I'm rubbing . . . what do you mean, you're on *Who Wants to Be a Millionaire*?'

'What am I doing? I'm cutting my toenails.'

'I'm Melody, I'm short and fat and I've lost most of my teeth.'

'You're being a very naughty boy . . . so I'm hanging up.'

'I'm Danielle, or Daniel, your choice.'

'Your call is very important to us, please continue to hold.'

'Press 1 for Northern, 2 for Brummie, 3 for an Essex slapper, otherwise please hold and take pot luck on whichever of our low-rent unattractive prostitutes becomes available first.'

UNLIKELY LINES FROM FAIRY TALES

And Cinderella and the prince lived happily ever after, until their carriage crashed in a Parisian road tunnel.

'Keep rubbing,' said the genie, 'and something magical will come out, if you know what I mean.'

'Old Mother Hubbard, we're from the NSPCC and we're acting on a tip-off.'

'Look, I know the duckling's different, but that's no excuse for calling him names, he's not ugly, he's just alternatively plumed.'

'Look, Snow White, it's great having you around, but this was only meant to be temporary so me and the lads think if you're going to stay you might have to start stumping up for the council tax.'

'Actually, Rapunzel, since you've had your Brazilian, there's much less for me to climb up.'

'Mr Bear, sorry to bother you, but we've had reports of an intruder in the area. You haven't noticed any porridge being taken have you?'

Tom Tom the piper's son, stole a pig and was beheaded live on Al Jazeera.

'Red Riding Hood, you are not going out dressed like that, you look like you're gagging for it.'

'There's been a terrible accident – is there a doctor with vinegar and brown paper?'

And Baby Bear said, 'Look who's sleeping in my bed – spread 'em, blondie.'

The third pig made his house out of bricks – which soon plummeted in value.

Tom Tom the piper's son – invented satnav.

Unfortunately, it was bad luck for Prince Charming, as when he woke up Camilla had turned back into an old boot.

'Meet my fellow dwarfs, Snow White: Anal, Oral, Doggy, Jizzy, Fisty and Bashful.'

Half a pound of tupenny rice – costs a billion dollars in Zimbabwe.

Humpty Dumpty had a great fall – remember, egg-based characters can go down as well as up.

UNLIKELY QUIZ SHOW QUESTIONS

'Let's have a look at what you could have won if you'd been on a better show.'

'How big is my cock?'

'The phone lines are open now with the question: how long will you be prepared to hold at £1.80 a minute?'

'The answers to those last questions were: cancer, and the Holocaust. Join us after the break when we'll be playing Pin the Jelly to the Wall.'

'What am I? No, it was a good guess, but 'a very lucky, talentless wannabe who has blow-jobbed his way to the top' is not the right answer.'

'Is this a question?'

'Are you gay? That's a question from your mum and dad, also signed by your wife.'

"Something you would keep secret from your wife.' You said, 'I shagged my sister at her fortieth birthday party.' Our survey said, 'You silly bastard, you weren't meant to be quite so specific."

'With reference to the criticism and the play itself, consider the ways in which the fascination of *Hamlet* depends on our tendency to identify with the character of Hamlet.'

'OK, and whoever is left unable to answer when the clock is ticking must eat the soggy biscuit, you know the rules.'

'You're watching Challenge TV, and you're playing for a jackpot of £1.50.'

'Dan, you are the weakest link. You were . . . shit – sorry, I've just run out of insults.'

'OK, your starter for ten: who is better, me or Bamber Gascgoine?'

'For ten points: is my career in the toilet?'

'Welcome to *The Weakest Link*. Your first question: do you fantasise about me in leather holding a whip?'

'Name something you'd find.'

'We asked you to complete the phrase: 'Hand –' for £50,000. None of you got the answer, which was 'Hand Amputation'.'

'If I said you had a beautiful body, would you hold it against me?'

'How small is too small?'

'Let's play *The Weakest Link*. What 'B' do I regularly inject into my forehead?'

'Complete the name of our double act: Ant and a) Dec, b) Dave.'

'You have two minutes on your specialist subject: the sex life of John Humphrys.'

'For a million pounds, what's the best way to cheat on *Millionaire*? Is it a) cough . . .'

'Okay, for a million pounds . . . I'm hosting this quiz show.'

'So, you have a choice of molecular physics, natural history or *Big Brother* winners.'

BAD THINGS TO HEAR ON A HOLIDAY PROGRAMME

'If, like me, you are just here for the sex tourism, wander down into the docks area around 9 p.m. to 4 a.m. any night.'

'You can actually have a pretty cheap holiday if you use a bit of nouse – for instance, you can get street children to carry you around in a sedan chair for a whole day, for just a couple of dollars.'

'If you're going to try and smuggle back drugs, shoving them up your rectum is probably the best bet.'

'The Rhine cruise is enjoyable, but be warned, it is full of Germans.'

'I'm Judith Chalmers and you may need to adjust the colour on your set.'

'. . . is one of the city's best restaurants and you can order most things without worrying you'll be puking and shitting like a two-way blender with no lid.'

'Don't drink the water and try not to get mugged – but once you're out of the UK you should be fine.'

'If you don't like people of other colours, then another option is the exclusive resort of Cape Blanco about fifty miles from here.'

'I lay there naked and warm until I was put back in economy class.'

'I'm standing in front of Delhi's newest big attraction, the Network Rail Call Centre.'

'The best thing about this country is the people. They all look so funny, don't they?'

'France is a country rich in culture, spoilt only by its people.'

'Tell the flight crew you've got a bomb in your luggage – there's nothing they like more than a good joke.'

'I'm afraid this is an economy flight, we don't have toilets – you'll have to shit in your seat.'

'Here's a tip if you're going to Faliraki – by mid season 90 per cent of the holiday reps will have herpes.'

'I'm lying here with a very large cocktail inside me . . . sorry, with a very large cocktail waiter inside me.'

'There are loads of activities here, which is just as well, as after a few problems at customs I haven't been able to sit down for four days.'

UNLIKELY THINGS TO SEE IN A SCHOOL ATLAS

The Xs are where I hid the bodies

Here be dragons

Bongo Bongo Land

All branches of Subway are marked with an S

My Mum's

The Lost City of Atlantis

Edge of the World where you'll fall off

Green represents apple production and red,
er, mass genocides

Britain may look bigger than normal on this map,
but that's because we're the best

All the countries marked in green are
where I've shagged a prozzie

This colour represents vomit on the streets

The closer the contours are together,
the more racist people are

If Italy's the leg then Spain must be the snatch

Atlas of the world in 300 million years' time:
as you can see, it's pretty much all blue

This atlas grades the women

This is the world as it would have been if
the beloved Führer had won

This is Ceylon, or Sri Lanka,
as we are supposed to bloody call it now

El Salvador: the El stands for Leonard

We have coloured these countries as to
how much of a shithole they are

That isn't a new island off Italy.
My son had a cold

UNLIKELY THINGS TO HEAR IN A PORN FILM

'There you go, Fräulein, I have fixed your dishwasher. Goodbye.'

'This blow job scene just doesn't seem to be essential to the plot.'

'Fuck! I think I've snapped my banjo string.'

'Is it in yet?'

'Is Pandora Peaks your real name?'

'I'm really annoyed that Tim Burton stole the plot of *Edward Penishands* and made his own version.'

'Sorry, love, it slipped up there by accident.'

'Sex? Is it my birthday?'

'Well, strictly missionary, turn the lights off and you can only do it through a hole in a sheet.'

'My contract says no nudity.'

'This has never happened to me before.'

'Is this based on a true story?'

'Your breasts look so real.'

POOR SUGGESTIONS FOR NEW OLYMPIC EVENTS

GRECO-ROMAN FOREPLAY

4X100M SHIT

HOP, SKIP AND MINCE

THE 3,000M PEOPLECHASE

BREASTSTROKE IN PYJAMAS WHILE CARRYING A BRICK

HUNTING WITH JAVELINS

RHYTHMIC SEXUAL INTERCOURSE

SPEED CRAPPING

OLD-FASHIONED PENTATHLON

BOLLOCK-NAKED VOLLEYBALL

CROSS-COUNTRY STREAKING

HAPPY SLAPPING

DRIVE-BY RIFLE SHOOTING

EGG AND SPOON RACE

SYNCHRONISED FLASHING

CROSS-CHANNEL BOOZING

SHIT PUT

LONG DUMP

HIGH PISS

THINGS THAT WOULD RUIN A MEAL IN A RESTAURANT

'Let me order for you, darling . . . The lady will have the cheapest thing on the menu, please.'

'This year we put our own excrement on the organic vegetable patch.'

'Is it me or does that sauce look like a burst abscess?'

'The next table said it's Mafia justice, but it'll be over soon.'

'I can see you were annoyed and I will replace your meal. Now, would you rather Chef spat, pissed or wanked in your soup?'

'That Casserole Cannibale was delicious, what was in it?'

'Would you like to choose a turkey for us to strangle for you?'

'Excuse me, waiter, it's my wedding anniversary today, so can you hurry up the service, I've got to get home to the wife . . .'

'We've roped that area off for the Hideous Skin Complaint Party.'

'Would Sir like to pull the sausage out of my arse now?'

'Here's the wine list, Sir, it's quite short: red, white or Blue Nun?'

'Are you the one who got me a written warning last week? Enjoy your steak.'

'I've got some spinach in my teeth – you don't mind if I take them out and clean them, do you?'

'No, I haven't farted, I have, in fact, shat myself.'

'Keep an eye out for Chef's blue elastoplast.'

'Mr Ramsay's coming to deal with your complaint personally.'

'Would you like to see our bulimic menu, Madam?'

'Help yourself at the salad bar – it's over there by the gents.'

'I couldn't help noticing Madam's backside as she walked in – are you sure you won't have the salad?'

'So, this peanut allergy of yours – how bad is it?'

'Each one of those apricots has been sucked by the chef and checked for flavour.'

UNLIKELY AIRCRAFT SAFETY ANNOUNCEMENTS

'Please fit your own oxygen mask before taking pleasure in the fruitless fight for breath of others.'

'Keep your seatbelt fastened at all times, though if we do crash, its only function will be to keep your body stationary as it burns.'

'The toilet is fitted with a smoke detector and also a hidden camera, for the enjoyment of Bernd, our chief air steward.'

'Your safety is our number one priority, obviously apart from our operating profit, which is secured by buying old reconditioned planes and cutting back on mechanical checks.'

'In the event of a serious incident, prayer sheets are found in your seat pocket and our in-flight crew are happy to dispense final sexual acts in the toilets to the front, middle and rear.'

'We'll now show you the procedure for a landing on water, but you don't have to bother watching this bit, because if we have to ditch in the Pacific you'll either die instantly or the sharks will get you.'

'The lifejacket can be located under your seat, as well as the stinking feet of the man behind you.'

'This is how you undo your seatbelt, although let's be honest, if you can't do this then you really shouldn't be on this plane in the first place.'

WORDS ALMOST NEVER FOUND IN ROMANTIC SONGS

CONSTIPATION

PROSTATE

SYPHILIS

CABBAGE

HACKSAW

DISCHARGE

RAY STUBBS

LARD

HAEMORRHOIDS

MUESLI

MUCUS

SLEET

PANTECHNICON

SMEGMA

THE M40

DR MENGELE

HERRING

UNLIKELY THINGS TO HEAR IN A WAR FILM

'Can you hear the drums, Fernando?'

'Yesterday I killed a man for the first time – it gave me a hard on.'

'Well, it started out as a tunnel, but since it's collapsed it's sort of become a grave for Ginger.'

'That's unlucky, parachuting out safely and landing on a pitch-fork.'

'Bad news, lads, the escape tunnel's come out in another prisoner of war camp.'

'All right, men, the night before the big push, why don't we all have a cuddle?'

'OK, men. We're about to go over the top. We can't help it with Daniel Day Lewis in the cast.'

'OK, men, first day of the Somme campaign. You go ahead without me, I've got a bit of a jippy tummy.'

'You know – in ten years' time our economy will have collapsed and Germany's will be the strongest in Europe.'

'I'll need some volunteers for this suicide mission. Well done, Ahmed.'

'Blowing up this dam is a vital mission – it will drain the entire reservoir and deny the Germans much-needed canoeing and water-skiing facilities.'

'Don't worry, the Belgian defences will hold them up – blimey, that was quick.'

'Ah, you must be the famous Douglas Bader. Don't get up.'

'The good news is we've blown the dam up, the bad news is that it was the Severn, not the Rhine.'

'I love the smell of napalm in the mornings – failing that, a freshly baked almond croissant and a latte.'

'Bad news, chaps – the Great Escape has failed. How about we try it again next Bank Holiday?'

'Er, Hannibal – you know those buns we were saving for when we got over the Alps . . . ?'

'Get me a shot of morphine. I haven't been injured, I just really want a shot of morphine.'

'Excuse me, Sergeant – this stretch of Western Front isn't nearly as quiet as I was led to believe.'

'Von Ryan's Express would like to apologize for the late running of this train.'

'I think Jerry is hiding behind that building. Fuck knows where Tom is, though.'

'So, the bullet bounced off the cigarette case in his breast pocket and ricocheted straight up into his brain.'

'I'm worried about our forger's eyesight. He's just made me this Deutsche Pissport.'

'You get in the plane and we'll catapult it off the roof. While the Germans are picking up the pieces of your body, we'll nip over the fence.'

THINGS TO SAY THAT WILL CHANGE THE ATMOSPHERE AT A DINNER PARTY

'I think I'm comfortably the richest person here.'

'That's it with just a semi on . . .'

'I know you're a granny now, but when you were young, did you like bum love?'

'Now, does everyone eat pig snout?'

'You know the bin Ladens, don't you, Mr Bush? Just don't mention 9/11, they're very touchy.'

'I've underestimated a little bit, so I'll have to give you a smaller portion, Mr Prescott.'

'Yes, I have got smallpox, but don't worry, if you've already had it you won't catch it.'

'Amy, they're here to take you back to rehab.'

'This is Pete Best, everyone, no jokes about the Beatles.'

'Anyone up for Islamic Pictionary?'

'Yes, I am that John Leslie.'

'Mmm, this satay nut roast is delicious – there aren't any nuts in it, are there?'

'My secret ingredient? I poach the fish in its own semen.'

'Before the cheese course we always pass round the smack.'

'No, I'll use the downstairs toilet, and leave the door open – that way we can carry on the conversation.'

'Are the Mafia still after you?'

'I am Mephisto and whoever ate the minestrone made a tacit bargain with me.'

'Have you met Lord and Lady Lucan?'

'Oh, that. That's just the volcano the house is built on.'

'There's a space over next to Heather, Sir Paul.'

'Can anyone else do this with their dick?'

Mr Andrews, there's a policeman to see you. I say policeman – it's more of an armed response unit.'

'Darling, are these the walnuts Johnny had up his nose?'

'Semen just tastes like humus.'

'Right, I'll go and fetch the fruit bowl, while you lot get your car keys out.'

'You've run out of toilet paper in your loo – so I used a towel.'

TEXT MESSAGES THEY JUST MISSED

This is the FIrsst evur t extmessage sent

Gordon, I'd call an election now if I were you, think the economy is going to go tits up. Love Tony

Romeo, am in the crypt but am not dead, just wait 4 me 2 wake up love Juliet xx

I'm still in that same cave just by the Khyber Pass – will be there until next Tuesday. Osama

Jon, you've left a CD-ROM with loads of personal details of benefit claimants in the pub

Mr al Fayed, we've just crashed in Paris, it was all an accident and by the way, I'm not pregnant or engaged, love Diana

Oedipus. She's your real mum mate. Oops bit late now. Lol. Polybus

Britney, you've forgotten your knickers, careful getting out of your car

Dear Mr Litvinenko. Tea and sushi meeting is off this morning

I'm texting you from the car behind, my brakes have failed and I can't slow down, get out of the wa . . .

Jesus, avoid the Garden of Gethsemane tonight, will explain later. Judas

THINGS TO SAY THAT WILL CHANGE THE ATMOSPHERE AT A DINNER PARTY

'How much money has everyone got in the bank?'

'Cerebral palsy? I thought you were just weird.'

'Whoever left that Stradivarius on the couch, I think one of the kids has just sat on it.'

'I wasn't, I was just stroking the dolphin's stomach.'

'Blindfold taste test – one of these is venison and one is human.'

'So, do you regret divorcing J. K. Rowling?'

'Funny, isn't it? The icing on here tastes like your husband's dick.'

'I think all policemen are Nazis. What do you do? Oh . . .'

'I always masturbate between first and second course, don't you?'

'I put on a film to keep the kids quiet – somebody with a deep throat or something.'

'No need to look at your shoes, it's me . . . I've shat myself.'

'The last time I was here I was searching your house with the vice squad.'

'Now, before we eat, Steven will choose one of you to be sacrificed to Satan.'

'More lattes? By the way, has anyone seen my breast milk?'

'And now with her tribute to Shirley Temple, our daughter . . .'

'You must be a wonderful teacher, Mrs Jones. Whenever Johnny talks about you he plays with himself.'

THINGS THAT WOULD RUIN A MEAL
IN A RESTAURANT

'Most amusing waiter joke, Sir – remind me which soup you were having.'

'Would Sir like to suck my knob now?'

'No, that isn't beetroot on your salad, Sir, it's the chef's blood.'

'Sorry, it's a bit undercooked, the chef is normally the washer-upper.'

'Three banoffee pies – I'll bring them after I've had a dump.'

[Fill in questionnaire:] Do *you* think we're unhygenic?

'The smelly old tramp on the next table sent over this bottle of meths for you.'

'Fillet of battery-farmed, bolt-killed Norfolk chicken.'

'Excuse me, ladies, I was just listening to your conversation, I wonder if you'd mind me silently masturbating?'

'We need the table back by 9 p.m., it's 8.54 now, so . . . two bananas and the bill?'

'No, it isn't sunburn, it's psoriasis.'

'Can anyone eating the lychee salad just stop for a moment? The chef has lost his false eye.'

'No, Sir, it's pig rectum, stuffed with goat's jizz on a bed of horse shit. We don't sell many, in fact you're the first person to order it.'

'It can be lethal if the chef doesn't cook it exactly right.'

'Unscrew my hand, I've got a bottle opener attachment.'

'Yes, I'll heat it up, down my trousers.'

'Waiter, have you got frog's legs?'
    'No, I'm disabled, you c*nt.'

'The only table left is very close to the toilets. In fact it's in a cubicle.'

'Sweetcorn and beetroot risotto – you'll be seeing that in every one of your shits this week, Sir.'

'It is self service. Chef, release the goose!'

'We'll have to sit you with the German naturist party.'

'We'll keep you under observation for an hour or so after you've finished and then you can go.'

UNLIKELY SMALL ADS

FOR SALE: Amuse your friends – tell them you paid £20 for this load of shit.

Write underwater with this bath, pen not included.

FOR SALE: pack of polos. Mint condition.

Formula One boss seeks Ein Deutsche Mädchen für grossen buttockslappen. Phone this number and ask for Granddad.

One aspirin for sale, 5p or nearest offer.

Be my mate and I'll spend millions on you every day. Robert Mugabe.

Bespectacled middle-aged *Star Trek* enthusiast seeks non-inflatable woman.

FOR SALE: one canoe, hardly used. Also – flat in Panama – genuine reason for sale – apply Durham Prison and ask for Stupid.

Recent divorcee WLTM rich sugar daddy to lavish gifts on me. I am blonde and leggy (one).

Real X-ray specs, apply Radiology Unit, Harefield Hospital. £500,000 o.n.o. (Not really specs, more of a room with big machine in it.) You didn't get it from me.

Series of golden arches collected over last decade not stolen from McDonalds at all, however it might look. £5 for the lot.

Bubbly fifty-something seeks man who likes fat grandmothers.

Soiled underwear from maximum-security mental institution, make me an offer.

Illegal pirate videos for sale, good quality apart from when that bloke in front gets up to go to the toilet in *Cloverfield*.

Canderel dispenser for sale, does not include Canderel.

Two cheeky, lovable Geordie TV stars, GSOH, why not phone us, calls will cost no more that £1 a minute.

Trunk full of Diana, Princess of Wales's belongings. Make me an offer. P Burrell (not that one).

Original Van Gogh for sale £50 million o.n.o. Frame not included, would make ideal present for someone who knows nothing about art and doesn't watch *Crimewatch*, slight rip in top corner.

Fresh manure for sale, loads of the stuff, £10 per bucket, buyer collects. P.S. Also plumber needed urgently.

Beautiful wife for sale, 40, blonde, curvaceous, would suit necrophiliac. Buyer collects.

UNLIKELY THINGS TO HEAR IN A WAR FILM

'Mission accomplished, Sir – as ordered, I've been shaving Ryan's privates.'

'Platoon! Phasers set to stun.'

'Tomorrow is the big push, men, and I've eaten a whole box of laxatives in preparation.'

'Ooh, I've ruined these trousers.'

'We're out of guns, Perkins, use this frisbee.'

'Watch out, Sergeant, he's wearing a rucksack.'

'I'll start the tunnel here, Cavendish, you start the covered walkway from the fourth floor.'

'Rommel, I didn't expect to see you in here and eating a family bucket.'

'I'm worried – now I've shown you a photograph of my wife and my farm back home, I don't think I'm going to make it.'

'OK, men, listen, this is what we're going to do: climb that wall, run along the top, cross the greasy bridge, shimmy up Nelson and ring the bell. The Germans will be throwing wet sponges at you.'

'You might be on to something here, Barnes Wallis – the bouncing plane, you say?'

'I do want to find Private Ryan, Sir, but I just can't take you seriously after *Forrest Gump*.'

UNLIKELY THINGS TO FIND WRITTEN ON TOILET PAPER PACKAGING

CHICKEN AND MUSHROOM FLAVOUR

BECAUSE YOU'RE WORTH IT

FEELS LIKE HAVING YOUR ARSE LICKED
BY A BIG SLOBBERY DOG

NO SALT ADDED

TESTED ON ANIMALS

GO BACK TO SCHOOL WITH NEW TRACING PAPER RANGE,
OR SEE WHAT YOU'RE DOING WITH NEW BACOFOIL BOG ROLL

SERVING SUGGESTION

DO NOT OPERATE HEAVY MACHINERY WHEN USING

SMOKING CAN DAMAGE YOUR HEALTH

DOES NOT CONTAIN NUTS

WILL EXPLODE ON CONTACT WITH WATER

RECYCLED – THAT'S WHY IT'S SUCH A FUNNY COLOUR

NEW ANAL EXCEL PHALLIC, CLEAN YOUR ARSE AND
BE ROGERED AT THE SAME TIME

REUSABLE

JUST ADD WATER

YOU CAN USE AS MANY CUTE PUPPIES AS YOU LIKE,
BUT ALL THIS DOES IS WIPE SHIT OUT OF
THE CRACK OF YOUR ARSE

UNLIKELY THINGS TO READ IN A RECIPE BOOK

Leave for thirty minutes, then add petrol.

Pour contents in, leave out and await botulism.

This will take at least nine hours to prepare, you might be better buying the same thing in Tesco.

Add the panda and, hey presto!

Mix carefully, holding nose and trying not to gag.

If at this point it has not risen, cancel dinner party.

Knead until hard, then ejaculate.

Do not operate heavy machinery with this meal.

Add cream, chocolate, stir, eat, vomit in toilets.

When baked hard, remove from oven and throw at husband.

Stir and stand on windowsill for an hour. No, not you, the fucking cake, dickhead!

A variation on his 'n' hers desserts – one for fat people and one for the normal.

Place both breasts onto worktop in order to distract dinner guests from the shit food.

Remove socks and wade around in it for a bit.

Leave to stand for at least six hours or so, then tape behind radiator, sell house, move, thus making it uninhabitable for the new owners.

Make sure you wash your hands thoroughly, especially if you've just had a really steamy, runny shit.

And if you can't find an apple to put in the pig's mouth, a budgerigar or hamster will suffice.

Ingredients: blood, semen and cheese of your choice.

Drain the blood, remove clothes, jewellery, dice and serve.

Best served between salad and dessert course when conversation has taken a racist turn.

Serves four, or one really greedy c*nt.

Add salt, vinegar, ketchup and eat.

Boil kettle, pour on, wait fifteen seconds, serve.

Ingredients: two bottles of vodka, ice, tonic water. On second thoughts, sod the tonic water, and actually the ice is optional as well.

Take a knob of butter (so that's between 1 and 14 inches, depending how much of a man you are).

Delia's recipe: add copious amounts of alcohol, wait forty-five minutes, take one microphone and then walk onto pitch at Carrow Road.

WEIRD THINGS TO HAVE TATTOOED ON YOUR ARSE

THIS IS MY ARSE

IF YOU ARE HERE FOR
ANY REASON OTHER THAN MEDICAL,
PLEASE CONSULT WITH THE OTHER END
AS A MATTER OF URGENCY

DO NOT OPEN IN PUBLIC

HOW DEEP IS YOUR LOVE?

HERE LIES FLUFFY, MUCH LOVED
AND MUCH MISSED GERBIL

30MPH SPEED LIMIT

DEAD END

CONCEALED ENTRANCE

FOR USE BY HER MAJESTY'S GOVERNMENT ONLY

NO KISSING, DIVING, RUNNING

LATHER, RINSE, REPEAT

UNNERVING THINGS TO HEAR IN A MEDICAL EXAM

'Can you cover one eye and read this in a sexy French accent?'

'I've run out of lubricant, so I'm going to spit on my finger.'

'I've never seen a shadow that big. Ah, panic over, there's a spider on the lens.'

'Nurse – the screens! The football's about to start.'

'I'm now going to num your vagina . . . num num num.'

'I think there is a clinic that can deal with an emergency like this, but it's in rural Japan.'

'Nurse, can you get the senior consultant, and tell him to run like fuck.'

'Can you climb up this ladder and shit into this bucket?'

'Well, I'm surprised, but I'm afraid you've got testicular cancer, Mrs Smith.'

'Just out of interest, do you have any favourite hymns or poems?'

'So, if you could just pop my clothes off . . .'

'Your bones appear to be made from a substance not known on this planet.'

'Yes, Siree, I taught myself all the fancy doctorin' I needs to know.'

'So, how bad is this premature . . . eeeeargh!'

'Aha, malignant. Yes! That's ten quid the radiologist owes me.'

UNLIKELY THINGS TO READ IN A RECIPE BOOK

Squeeze cheese out of tube and on to cracker. Spread.

Completed meal will bear no resemblance to picture.

Take one raw, still-beating pig's heart.

If you can't get Sevruga caviar, fish paste will do just as well.

Remove penis, wipe on curtains. Light cigarette, go to sleep.

After three hours, open the oven, realize you're two hours too late, and phone for a pizza.

For a less fattening version of this dessert, don't eat so much of it.

Then add the eye of toad, and leg of newt, and leave to hubble and bubble for 15 minutes.

I love to scoop up the last traces of this naughty sauce straight from the bowl, and then lick my fingers suggestively, while I'm being fucked across the kitchen table.

Smooth the icing, now remove your pants and sit on it till done.

Take the chicken kievs out of the freezer, then peer at them closely, and guess whether the sell-by date says 09 or 00.

And, hey presto, a perfect lemon jizz cake!

Take your very sharpest sushi knife and very carefully creep up behind your cheating bastard of a husband.

Mince, pour, serve – is all you need to do as a cocktail waiter.

Rinse. Lather. Repeat.

CELEBRITY SCENTS YOU'LL NEVER SEE

PRINCE HARRY'S SURPRISINGLY GINGER

ARMAGEDDON BY AHMADINEJAD

VACANT BY DAVID BECKHAM

GARY GLITTER'S TOUCH OF CHILDREN

HINT OF TALENT BY VICTORIA BECKHAM

WAYNE ROONEY'S VIEUX FEMME

PIERS MORGAN'S SMUG

PETER CROUCH'S STREAK OF PISS

AGYNESS DEYN'S POINTLESS

HOT AIR FROM BORIS JOHNSON

NIL BY WINEHOUSE

VOMIT FROM GAZZA

DESPERATION FROM GORDON BROWN

RUSSELL BRAND'S INDISCRETION

SHAMELESS BY STRINGFELLOW

KEIRA KNIGHTLEY'S IRRITATING

UNLIKELY THINGS TO READ IN A SCHOOL FRENCH BOOK

If Mademoiselle Fifi can entertain three gentlemen an hour, how much can she make in a day?

Everyday French Situations Exercise 4: Signing for Arsenal.

Et maintenant, l'histoire de le battle de Agincourt.

Write an essay on President Sarkozy without mentioning his wife's baps.

Here are Monsieur Vernier, Madame Vernier, and Granddad Vernier, who collaborated during the war.

Remember – if during your French exam you don't know an answer, just shrug your shoulders and go, 'Pffff.'

Once you have learned French, you will be able to read Proust, Jean-Paul Sartre, and listen to French opera in the original language. But it's not all bad news.

Chapters 18–39: The Rules of Boules.

If you must set fire to British lamb, please wait until the lorry is out of the Channel Tunnel.

Write a letter to your French pen pal, Hélène, telling her about yourself, where you live and encouraging her to send back photographs of herself in her underwear.

Napoleon was a silly little twat. Discuss.

There is no French word for Ladyshave, deodorant or fighting till the last man.

Translate the following sentence: 'Why bother to learn French? They all speak English anyway.'

True or false? France has given the world great pop music.

Useful French phrases:

'What cheese is this?'

'This is nice cheese.'

'Where is the cheese?'

'Can I have some more cheese?'

'I admire this cheese, I like a strong cheese.'

'Do you mind if I just hold your cheese?'

'At home I have five different cheeses.'

'Can I see the cheese board please?'

'You have a lovely selection of cheese.'

'Hey you, get off of my cheese.'

'President de Gaulle was a great Frenchman and he liked cheese a lot.'

'Have you only got fucking cheese?'

UNSUCCESSFUL JOB APPLICATIONS

I love all animals, especially with mustard.

I won't travel.

Deer Surr or Madum . . .

I am both lazy and a miserable git.

Qualifications: 7 ASBos, endorsed driving licence, restraining order.

I am an ambitious, motivated, rampant homosexual.

I have a phobia of desks and computers.

I worked as a web designer on the now defunct sites LustyLolitas.com and UnderagePussy.co.uk.

It has always been my dream to work as a sandwich maker in Subway.

Name: Sutcliffe, Peter
Job history: 1977–1981 Lorry driver.
1981–2008: errm, doing A levels, I now have 113.
I like to set myself goals and never fail to miss.

I have attention deficit disorder, Tourette's, body odour and love dogging.

I have just come back from a 23-year senten– sorry, spell in Vietnam.

I would like to work for your company to pay the bills and hopefully use colleagues for casual sex until I find a better-paid and more enjoyable position.

I am an ambitious, conscientious, hardworking, curvy blonde who is up for anything.

I don't work well on my own or as part of a group.

I like to see myself as a 'people person'; others use the term 'rapist'.

I worked as a strategist for Northern Rock, Enron and Mayor Ken's campaign team.

Employers 2001–2006: Al Qaeda.
Reference: Mr O. bin Laden, Cave 6, Jihad Road, Kandahar, Afghanistan.

My name is Steve McClaren and I would love to be manager of your international football team.

I would be ideal for the vacancy at your company because I have not worked since 1976.

I have considerable experience working with spazzers.

Gizza job, go on, I can do that.

LINES YOU NEVER HEAR IN THE SOAPS

'Oi, Peggy, I can't drink this, your bra has just twanged off and landed in my pint.'

'Harold, guess what: the government have decided to hand Ramsay Street back to the Aborigines.'

'Ricky, get in here quick, we're on telly, having this conversation.'

'Dot, if you sold your house in Albert Square, you'd be able to buy a nice place in the country.'

'You know, for a small street in a quiet suburb of Manchester, there's an incredible turnover of people.'

'I'm fed up of the Queen Vic, let's go somewhere else.'

'I'm sorry, you're too old, fat and dark-haired to live in Hollyoaks.'

'Isn't it incredible that whenever you open the door to go out in Ramsay Street, someone is always standing there?'

'I had a car crash because we needed to use the Erinsborough Hospital set again.'

'I'm really annoyed with you. Let's go over to the Queen Vic and have a huge row in front of everyone.'

'So, that's resolved everything and everyone's fine.' (B-Dum Dum dum dum dum)

'Bad news about the band we've booked for the wedding. Only the drummer's turned up.' (B-Dum Dum dum dum dum)

'Oh, no! The synth drum's broken!' (B-Dum–)

'Oh, Phil, I'm so proud of you, becoming Walford's first BNP councillor.'

'We don't need to talk.'

'Hey, guys, are we in *Neighbours* or *Home and Away*?'

'What we need is some sort of transparent gimmick to make this end on a spurious moment of suspense.'

'This is the fucking East End, I'll fucking swear if I fucking want to.'

'Blimey, doesn't anyone in Albert Square own a washing machine?'

'Poor old Dot, she seems to be going through some pseudo-psychological existential crisis . . .'

'The Queen Vic's changed management. It's now a gay pub.'

'Phil, I'm leaving the Arches, I've finally got funding for my PhD.'

UNNERVING THINGS TO HEAR IN A MEDICAL EXAM

'If you could just pop your clothes off in time to this music and look into the camera.'

'I'm just looking into your ear and . . . what's this? A pound coin? A bunch of flowers? A dove?'

'Your penis is a perfectly normal size . . . if you were a vole.'

'OK, your breasts look fine. Would you like to see my cock in exchange?'

'Now, what seems to be the . . . fucking hell!'

'Just one moment, Mr Johnson . . . Hello, is that Channel 5? I think I've got another documentary idea for you.'

'Eurgh, I'm not touching that.'

'We are going to test your reflexes and practise my knife-throwing act at the same time.'

'I'm afraid it's bad news, you've got . . . oh hang on, there's the phone, can I take this? Yes, hi, this won't take long will it? Only I'm with a patient and she might not make it to the end of this call.'

'Brian, you've got to come and see this!'

'I'm afraid you've got Parkinson's Disease. This means you'll start interviewing people . . . only kidding, no, you've got Parkinson's.'

'It can't be what it looks like – you can only get it if you've shagged a dog . . . why are you crying?'

'Can I get a picture? I'm doing a book on freaks.'

'Everyone, clear. I've just farted.'

'You need to take a spoonful of semen every day – 4 p.m. is best for me . . .'

'There's something wrong with your clitoris but I can't quite put my finger on it.'

'I'm going to need a second opinion, because I'm not actually a doctor.'

'Stand back, nurse, I'm going to pop it.'

'Right, Mrs Jones, if you could just take your bra off we'll have a look at that ingrowing toenail of yours.'

'Now we're going test your sphincter control.'

'Close your eyes, open your mouth and start sucking when I give the signal.'

UNLIKELY SMALL ADS

WANTED: Gullibility test kit – send £19.99 now!

Wedding dress for sale, size 36, unused – slight éclair stains on front.

Portfolio of shares for very quick sale. £500 o.n.o.

Wanted: undroppable soap. Contact G. Glitter.

Tickets for Ben Elton musical – genuine reason for sale: it's shite.

WANTED: swear box. Industrial size, min. 8 cubic metres. Apply G. Fucking Ramsay.

Condom for sale – slight tear. Rinse thoroughly.

Limited-edition 'Diana Crash' memorial plate for sale. Slightly chipped.

Holiday to Ayia Napa – price includes accommodation, food, drink and STD treatment.

NOT WANTED: cleaner/housekeeper, apply Tracey Emin.

Lost in London: container of polonium-210. If found, please contact Vlad on Moscow-312456.

FOR SALE: Unwanted Christmas present – one gold-plated leg inscribed *To Heather with Love*.

Nude painting of a young Cherie Blair, make me an offer, please.

Heir to the crown turning sixty, seeks assassin for urgent job.

SWF, GSOH seeks extra vowels for good scrabble score.

Technophobic? Simply download our helpful podcast at www.technophobe.com

Box of finest Havana cigars – slightly damp. Contact B. Clinton.

Titanic memorabilia – perfectly preserved underwater. Buyer collects.

Radical imams required. Must have GSOH and own hook.

Injured at work? Want to sue your boss? Then fuck off to America.

Struggling with lots of small debts? Why not consolidate them into one impossibly huge debt?

Stop snoring – fast! – with this kitchen knife. Stab your husband and say goodbye to nocturnal rumble-misery for ever!

FOR SALE: one stick of dynamite, used.

Suspiciouslycheaptickets.com – we fly you to within 200 miles of where you want to go.

THINGS YOU WON'T HEAR ON BREAKFAST TV

'WAKEY WAKEY! Come on, get up, you're going to miss your bus. Come on, don't make me come up there! This is what happens when you go to bed as late as that. Get up, you lazy bastard!'

'Morning, Britain, bloody hell, you look like I feel.'

'And now your chance to win £10,000 with Keith Chegwin – will he stick his cock through your letterbox?'

'I'm not saying I'm tired, but the bags under my eyes look like scrotums.'

'And now, over from America, a guest I give a fuck about.'

'I'll now interview another nutter with a mad theory for the next ten minutes, not because he's any good, but we can never get people in this early.'

'It takes me more time to look like this than it took John Hurt to get made up for *The Elephant Man*.'

'I get up at 2 a.m. every day, I'm on the edge, yesterday I killed a man.'

'Here's some footage of my stomach band being fitted.'

'Now the news where Penny Smith will try and be funny.'

'Hey, call in sick, there's some great stuff on later, porn and every-thing.'

'Morning, Britain, I had a cracking vindaloo last night, good job it isn't smellovision.'

'If you've just woken up with an erection, here's Suzy with the weather.'

'I haven't been to bed!!!'

'It's six o'clock, I haven't had time for a shower and my tights are stuck to me.'

'I get up at 3 a.m. every day for this job and I wonder why my wife's fucking the postman.'

'And now, Lorraine Kelly will attempt to conduct an interview without telling her guest they 'look gorgeous' or using the word 'boobies'.'

'So now let's have a look at the new haemorrhoid cam.'

UNLIKELY SMALL ADS

I'm a 14-year-old girl looking for a 45–55 man for online webcam fun. Email me: operationlolita @metpolice.uk.

91-year-old man seeks erection. Can you help?

Gay man seeks female for ongoing parental charade.

Narcissistic, masochistic, schizophrenic hypochondriac seeks good listener.

Masochist seeks same for emotional stand-off.

I was the tall, striking redhead on the District Line who got off at Turnham Green, you were the bearded man with the dog, sunglasses and white stick I was blowing kisses at. Call me.

FOR SALE: binoculars and gloves. Unwanted gifts. Apply Abu Hamza.

Have entire set of *Two Pints of Lager and a Packet of Crisps* DVDs. Will swap for half-eaten can of baked beans. o.n.o.

Want a Thai bride? Visit us on nastysurpriseon weddingnight.com.

WANTED: rubber bedsheet. Apply A. Winehouse.

Keep cats out of your garden with these pressure activated land mines.

Giant pyramid for sale in Giza, buyer collects.

Fool burglars with our baked bean tin that's actually a storage box. So realistic, you'll throw it away for recycling and lose your life savings.

Want somewhere to put all your 1p coins? Buy this 1p piggy bank for £10.99.

Finish your series of Christopher Biggins wall-mounted china plates with number five: 'The Rentaghost Years'.

Turn your shoes into fashionable crocks with our exclusive hole puncher.

Here's the ideal present for dads and uncles: a completely trained, fully washable Eastern European au pair.

Feel like Bruce Parry with our one-size-fits-all tribal penis gourd.

WANTED: new iconic female victim for *Daily Express* front page.

Watch how to make thousands quickly with my easy-to-follow course. Send me £1,000 for part one.

Bright copper kettles, warm woollen mittens, brown paper packages tied up with string; 10% off some of your favourite things.

Gillian McKeith's healthy chocolate log with nut and corn, ideal for the Christmas table.

THINGS YOU DON'T WANT TO HEAR
IN A PSYCHIATRIST'S OFFICE

'What you made there was what we call a Freudian cock – I mean slip.'

'Hello? Hello?! What sort of a greeting is that? You're obviously a closet homosexual with an Oedipus complex.'

'You think you've got troubles . . .'

'I insist on all my female patients taking their tops off. Flb lb lb lb.'

'I'll need to strap you in for this one.'

'I'll have to hurry you, I'm seeing a Mr Bonaparte at two o'clock.'

'Your mother's quite a fox – I'm not surprised you want to shag her.'

'Look at this inkblot of two lesbians doing it and tell me what you see.'

'Deny it all you like, I can tell you fancy me.'

'Sorry, you're not allowed up on the couch.'

'If you feel a bump – that'll be my erection.'

'I'd like to analyse your dreams – but only the filthy ones.'

'Never mind about your childhood.'

'Well, I don't get many eighteen-year-old blondes who try and cure me of their sexual – oh, I've come.'

'You're what we psychiatrists refer to, technically, as a 'fruitcake'.'

'You lie on the couch, which I've just noticed resembles a giant penis.'

'I think I can diagnose your condition – you're mental.'

'No, no, keep talking – my iPod's playing up.'

'Tell me your sexual hang-ups again, Miss Jones – only more slowly and in time with my right hand. I'll just get some tissues.'

'The good news is that you are perfectly sane, the bad news is that I'm mad as a hatter.'

'We'll try word association. I'll say a word and you say the first thing that comes into your breasts.'

'OK, I'm going to show you some objects, what do they make you think of? The first one is . . . my penis.'

'Well, I've read all of Freud, although admittedly I mean Clement.'

'Sane? You've just paid me £300 for the last hour.'

'You don't have to be mad to come here, but you are.'

UNLIKELY FRONT-PAGE HEADLINES

'YOU'RE ALL C*NTS' SAYS QUEEN

CROSSRAIL TUNNEL UNCOVERS
DOOR TO HELL

CLIMATE IS FUCKING FUCKED SAYS AL GORE

BROWN, BORIS & CAMERON SEX TAPE
– AMAZING PICS

ELVIS FOUND READING LE NEWS
ON FRENCH TV

BUSH CONVERTS TO ISLAM

BLUNKETT: I COULD SEE ALL ALONG

OI AFRICA! USE JOHNNIES! SAYS POPE

GOOGLE BOUGHT BY GINSTERS

SHARK BIT OFF MY HEAD AND I LIVED

MEN ARE LITERALLY FROM MARS,
WOMEN ARE LITERALLY FROM VENUS
SAYS DRAMATIC NEW STUDY

ALL PROBLEMS IN WORLD SOLVED

DRINK 16 BEERS A DAY SAY DOCTORS

NOT MUCH HAPPENING REALLY

OBAMA IN TOE STUB HORROR!
'OW' SCREAMS HOPPING PRESIDENT

FUCK YOU

IS THIS THE MYTHICAL LAND OF
'AUSTRALIA'? EXCLUSIVE PICTURES

OOH, MY LUNCH IS
REPEATING ON ME A BIT

CHARLES CONSTRUCTS CHEESE VILLAGE
IN CORNWALL

UNLIKELY THINGS TO HEAR ON
ANTIQUES ROADSHOW

'Well, Sir, it's absolutely incredible, I have to admit I've rarely seen one as large or well preserved as that, but if you could put it away now and show us your antique?'

'Today you join us at the Winston Silcott Youth Centre in Brixton.'

'Now then, now then, these are the Duchess's clothes, kept them in my wardrobe, you see.'

'It's been in the family about errm . . . four minutes . . . I saw it sticking out of that old man's rucksack.'

'What you have here is an old Victorian sex toy. Do you still use it?'

'It's fucking worth more than that.'

'I'm not sure they had *GuitarHero* in the eighteenth century.'

'Yes, it's an original Rembrandt, but it's probably only worth, um, a fiver. Would you, er, like me to, er, take it off your hands?'

'Yes, I got given this ceremonial sceptre when I became Prince of Wales. It's been in the family since the War of the Roses, what's it worth? I need the cash, the organic biscuit market's gone tits up.'

'There's loads more where this come from, mate, mum's the word.'

'These are the clothes from my mother – I'm telling him, I'm telling him, mother.'

'Well, let's have a look at him . . . I think he's worth quite a lot of money, but all I know is he's very old, not in very good condition and is married to Catherine Zeta Jones.'

'I actually got it from my father, along with chlamydia.'

'And if you notice this little insignia down here on the base . . . it says IKEA.'

'Cut the crap, mate, how much is it worth and do you want to buy it? I've got other people interested.'

'Its origins are uncertain but it's been with the same family for more than twenty years – a bit like Prince Harry.'

'What a piece of shit.'

'Yes, it's an urn containing the ashes of Arthur Negus.'

'Oh dear, you ain't paid us this month Miss Bruce, have you? That's a nice vase, be a real shame if someone dropped it, oopsy daisy, I'm feeling clumsy, oh dear, oh dear.'

UNLIKELY THINGS TO HEAR FROM A WEATHER FORECASTER

'Today mostly dry with some wet patches, but enough about my trousers.'

'So, Thursday and Friday mild and warm, Saturday an asteroid will hit the Irish Sea and destroy the Earth. That's it from me, bye bye.'

'What are you watching me for? Just go and look out of the window.'

'Tomorrow it'll be wetter than my wife's knickers on our wedding night.'

'And following today's rain of blood, tomorrow doesn't look any better, with a plague of locusts moving in from the west.'

'It'll be shitting it down until Wednesday night.'

'And there's my house where, over the weekend, it'll be raining men. Hallelujah!'

'And for those of you, like me, who had a bet on a white Christmas, there was definitely snow on the roof of the Met Office and I don't care if the bookies make out it wasn't anywhere else, I need that money.'

'Further north it will be wet, moist, damp, juicy, lubricated, oozing, unctuous, mmm . . . yes there . . . mmm, that's it, keep going, sorry, um, showers moving from the west should be clear by Tuesday.'

'And if we look at the satellite picture, we can clearly see Iran's nuclear facility, despite what Ahmadinejad says.'

'Clouds here, storms here and, what's this? Oh God, it's . . . oh, I see, someone has just sneezed on the monitor.'

'And as you can see, I can put my head here and completely obscure Yorkshire. If only it were possible to do that in real life.'

'And as for Thursday, if we just have a look at our seaweed, it's mainly dry with occasional showers and 17 degrees.'

'And if we take a quick look at the map I can clearly see we should have taken that turning an hour ago but, oh no, Mr Macho knew the way, he knew better, wouldn't stop and ask, oh no . . .'

'Tomorrow, it'll be bright and sunny . . . BECAUSE I HAVE COMMANDED IT, AND I AM THE GOD OF WEATHER. BOW DOWN, FOOLISH MORTALS!'

'And as we look . . . where's Scotland gone? Fuck!'

'Thunderbolt and lightning, very very frightening me . . . Galileo, Galileo Figaro, magnificoooo . . . '

'And so, as we can see, for the next few days it'll be dark, icy and treacherous, much like the relationship between me and my wife.'

'Moving our satellite pictures on, let's take a look at the weather in Oman, like any of you give a fuck, what's the betting it's really sunny and dry? Well, bugger me, it is . . . that useful to all of you in Guildford?'

'And if I put these two clouds closer together and add a snow symbol, see if you think, as I do, that it looks like a fat naked woman bending over a unicorn? Do you see it there, yeah?'

UNLIKELY COMPLAINTS TO THE BBC

Dear BBC, I am a huge fan of *Only Fools and Horses* and my friend told me of a hilarious bit where Del falls through a wine bar counter. I've never seen it and don't believe it exists. Can you show it, please?

Dear BBC, I'm a middle-aged white male, degree educated. Where are *my* fucking programmes?

Dear BBC, as a music fan, I find it deeply frustrating that I have to sit through twenty-nine minutes of whining cockney misery before hearing a brief snatch of decent eighties synth drums.

Dear BBC, I write to you but you never write to me.

Dear BBC, I'm a little unhinged – if you read this letter out I'll kill myself.

Dear BBC – everything on ITV, eh? It's shite.

Dear *Points of View*, is it true some of your letters are made up by us researchers here in the production office?

Dear BBC, can you warn us in advance if Andrew Lloyd Webber is about to appear on screen? A red triangle, perhaps?

Dear BBC, could you explain the plot of last week's *Murder, She Wrote*? It moved at too fast a pace for me.

Dear BBC, regarding *Can't Cook, Won't Cook* – they Can, and they Do.

Dear BBC, what has happened to that nice Jill Dando? She's been off our screens far too long.

Dear BBC, much as I enjoyed last night's *Nigella Express*, I must say the food somewhat detracted from her stupendous waps.

Dear BBC, while watching Road Runner I was appalled at the continuing plugs for Acme products. Is this the correct use of licence payers' money?

Dear BBC, have you ever thought of bringing back *Doctor Who*?

Dear BBC, what's wrong with the British public? They just fill up the airwaves with their constant moaning. I can't stand it. I mean in my day, we just watched the TV and if we didn't like it we just had to put up with it. We were lucky to have one. I mean the kids today, don't get me started, with their mobile phones, their games consoles and their funny accents, I just don't understand them. Mind you, my wife doesn't understand me. I'd have had an affair but I can't get an erection and I've got uncontrollable flatulence and halitosis. This is terrible at parties, not that we get invited out ever or if we do not with anyone I'd actually want to spend any time with. Ooh, I've got a funny pain down my right arm, they're saying it's not a heart thing, but then what do you expect from the bloody NHS. They just don't want me to come in and use a bed. God forbid I should actually use something I pay my taxes for. I never go in there except when my old mum died on a trolley in A&E, misdiagnosis my arse. Two hours she was there in a puddle of her own piss, I mean I'm not one to moan, but . . .

UNLIKELY SMALL ADS

Phone for sale – call this number. If someone answers, it's already gone.

WANTED: human guinea pig, for family pet.

For Sale: 4,996-piece jigsaw. No corners.

Call our sex line now – and ask a fat, ugly, middle-aged woman what colour knickers she's wearing.

Broken vase. One careful owner.

Original Rembrandt. £20 million, or nearest offer. Cash only for quick sale.

For Sale: fully working torture rack, with spiked mask and iron ankle restraints. Unwanted gift.

Slightly rusty but much-loved needles – apply P. Doherty.

LOST: marbles. If found, please return to T. Cruise, Hollywood.

FOR SALE: rocket-powered car, three miles on clock, apply R. Hammond.

Trainee Swedish topless masseuse seeks flabby, middle-aged male to practise on. Will happily give sex in payment.

Taxi drivers needed; clean driving licence and knowledge of local area not required.

FOR SALE: one large tin, silver polish. Never used. Apply T. Henman.

Sperm clinic needs donors – please come quickly.

Want to make thousands of pounds fast? Tell me about it!

Baggage handlers required – £6 per hour, plus all the stuff you can nick.

ODD-JOB MAN: bricklaying, plastering and gynaecology.

Your name written on a grain of rice – no job too small.

Confused gay guy would like to meet similar. I enjoy naked fishing and being President of Russia.

Piping hot showers at any time of the day? Let me piss on you.

Complete collection of *Tomorrow's World* series. Only available on Betamax.

500 pairs of shoes, worn once or not at all. Apply any woman.

Tin of chewy toffee, no use to owner. Apply Shane MacGowan, the Arches, Waterloo Embankment.

WANTED: metal dustbin lid. Must be sturdy. Apply Beagle 2, British Mars project.

Madame Zara sees the future. You will NOT ring 020 6014 6056.

UNLIKELY TV LISTINGS

9.00 a.m. Make Me an Egghead
Dermot Murnaghan performs brainwashing and plastic surgery on members of the public to make them terminally dull.

9.30 a.m. Cops, Cops, Cops
Fantastically cheap-to-make programme where policemen and women put on an act for the cameras and let black people go with a cheery word of warning.

11.00 a.m. The C*nty Wanky Tits show
Cutting-edge comedy on Channel 4 hosted by Mark Dolan and an 8 ft rubber vagina.

12.00 p.m. Egyptian Nazi Sharks II
Channel 5's popular documentary series returns.

12.30 p.m. Titchmarsh
Alan takes things too far with guest Rebecca Loos and a set of ping-pong balls.

1.00 p.m. Meerkats Under the Hammer
Tragic mix-up in the BBC daytime commissioning department results in a grisly, yet watchable half hour.

2.00 p.m. Midsomer Sexual Assaults
Late-night version of the popular ITV show. Barnaby is called to the aftermath of a gay toga party in a beautifully restored Jacobean manor house.

3.00 p.m. Celebrity Come Drink with Me
Peter O'Toole mixes a bucket of cocktails for Gazza, Mel Gibson, Amy Winehouse and Lindsay Lohan.

4.00 p.m. Not Going Out
Since the BBC cancelled it.

5.00 p.m. Diagnosis Nepotism
Starring Dick van Dyke, Barry van Dyke, Jenny Harris-van Dyke and Oliver van Dyke. Directed by Mary van Dyke.

6.00 p.m. The Real George Michael
Investigative reporter Jacques Peretti travels the world and discovers George Michael is both a homosexual and a user of the drug cannabis.

6.30 p.m. Murder Connections
Doon Mackichan voices a look at all the various movers and shakers involved in Lord Lucan's nanny's death and the peer's subsequent escape.

7.00 p.m. The Lost Poems of Abu Yaere
BBC4 documentary with more people working on it than will ever watch it.

7.30 p.m. Ivy League Angst
Film that doesn't translate for a British audience at all but is worth seeing basically because you get to see Natalie Portman's baps about thirty-five minutes in.

8.00 p.m. Imagine
Alan Yentob spends a week with Keith Chegwin to uncover the man behind the genius.

9.00 p.m. Celebrity Fonejacker
Russell Brand and Jonathan Ross ring up celebrities for a laugh.

9.30 p.m. Jeremy Clarkson Saves the Environment
New fifteen-part series. Jeremy hovers over a rainforest in a private jet to examine the damage done to the Amazon, with special guests the Bangkok Ping-Pong Ball Orchestra.

10.00 p.m. Celebrity How to Look Good Naked
Gok meets Ann Widdecombe.

11.00 p.m. Prince Harry's Pakistan
This week the ginger royal narrowly avoids starting a war.

11.30 p.m. World Crossword Championships
Ray Stubbs and Hazel Irvine present the afternoon's second round, live and uninterrupted from Aylesbury Library.

12.00 a.m. This Morning
Hosted by Chris and Ingrid Tarrant for as long as possible, until one of them storms off set.

1.30 a.m. Shitcom
The writers of *Teenage Kicks* and *The World According to Bex* join up with the team behind *Life of Riley* to try and reach a new low in televised comedy. Starring Caroline Quentin, Nicholas Lyndhurst and Blakey from *On the Buses*.

2.00 a.m. River Factory Cookbook
A series of microwave recipes for battery-farmed chickens.

3.00 a.m. Tom's Shoes
Soap set in a small shoe shop in Hemel Hempstead.

4.00 a.m. The South Bank Show
Melvyn Bragg profiles the comedian Norman Collier.

WEIRD THINGS TO HAVE TATTOOED ON YOUR ARSE

VOTE LIB DEM

OPEN OTHER END

BEWARE: HAZCHEM

ABANDON HOPE ALL YE WHO ENTER HERE

SUITABLE FOR LONG VEHICLES

THIS CAN BE SEEN FROM SPACE

OW!

IF YOU CAN READ THIS,
YOU'RE FAR TOO FUCKING CLOSE

BOY GEORGE RESIDED HERE 1986–1988

WARNING: FALLING SHIT

HONK BEFORE YOU BONK

MAXIMUM WIDTH: 18 INCHES

WISH YOU WERE HERE

GIVE WAY

CARDS YOU NEVER SEE IN A NEWSAGENT'S WINDOW

COME IN AND 'BROWSE'

BIRTHDAY CARD FOR SALE,
WOULD SUIT SOMEONE CALLED KEN.

BONA FIDE JULIUS CAESAR'S
ORIGINAL LATIN DICTIONARY FOR SALE.
CAVEAT EMPTOR.

KNITTER? PERVERT? COME TO THE
STITCH 'N' FIST AT THE VILLAGE HALL,
THURSDAY NIGHTS 8 P.M.

VILLAGE WEIRDO AVAILABLE FOR
HOME VISITS, CHILDREN'S PARTIES
AND BUS-SHELTER LOITERING.
CONTACT VIA INTERNET 24/7.

VILLAGE BIKE FOR SALE.
GOES WELL. NEEDS OILING. BUYER COLLECTS.
ANSWERS TO THE NAME OF 'GILLIAN'.

ME: 45, 6FT, SINGLE PROFESSIONAL, GSOH,
LOVES GARDENING, CLASSICAL MUSIC
AND TELLING PEOPLE ABOUT MYSELF.

UNLIKELY FRONT-PAGE HEADLINES

READERS OF THIS PAPER ARE IDIOTS, SAYS POLL

AT LAST! ANN WIDDECOMBE TOPLESS

COMPLICATED STOCK EXCHANGE FRAUD
– FULL DETAILS INSIDE

MY INCREDIBLE 45 MINUTES EACH WAY
WITH SUPER STUD PHIL NEVILLE

GEORGE MICHAEL IS GAY – FAKE SHEIKH EXPOSÉ

LOTS OF ANTS FOUND IN THE WORLD

JFK DEAD – OFFICIAL

FREDDIE STARR ATE MY HAM

FREE INSIDE: 'WOMEN OF THE CABINET'
CHARITY CALENDAR

GOTCHA! MAN CAUGHT SPEEDING ON MOTORWAY

SOME TRAINS DELAYED . . . A BIT

DIANA ENQUIRY LATEST

DYSLEXIC TYPESETTER GIVEN THE SOCK

FUCK! WAR!